I0102555

JUSTICE 3

SUN OF A GUN

❦

SA'ID SALAAM

URBAN AESOP PUBLICATIONS

Copyright © 2021 by Sa'id Salaam

All rights reserved.

No part of this book may be reproduced in any form or by any electronic or mechanical means, including information storage and retrieval systems, without written permission from the author, except for the use of brief quotations in a book review.

Email: Saidmsalaam@gmail.com

Cover Designer: Adriane Hall

Proofread: KaiCee White

Proofread: Brandi Jordan

Book Formatting: Tisha Andrews

PROLOGUE

"Car approaching," one of the security guards radioed to the other and took aim through the scope of her rifle.

"I'm on him," the other announced and took aim through his own scope. The driver didn't see them but knew they were there. He rolled down his window and extended a white flag to show he came in peace.

"Could be a trick," the female said and tightened her finger on the trigger.

"It's Sun!" little Killa said when he recognized one of his beloved big brothers and lowered his gun.

"Could be a trick!" Diedra insisted and kept her weapon trained.

"Don't shoot!" Sun said in each direction with his hands raised above his head. He didn't know where his siblings were perched but he was sure they were out there. His hands were high but Diedra still fired a shot. "Ouch! Stop shooting! Ma! Ouch! Come get, ouch, your daughter!"

"Stop shooting your brother lil girl!" Yolo fussed as she came out on the front porch.

"Told you not to buy them those BB guns," Killa said, shaking his head. He was aging quite nicely for a fifty something year old. Even with the grey in the temples and rounded belly of a happy spouse, happy house.

"Mom, dad," Sun greeted and hugged his parents. Paradise lays at the feet of mothers so he started with her. Once he hugged them both he backed off to share the good news. "Mom, dad, I met a girl!"

"A what?" Yolo asked and looked around fearfully.

"Don't say that too loud. She, might hear you." Killa whispered urgently and looked around as well.

"I'm not afraid of Shyne!" Sun declared but he still looked down the driveway to make sure her car wasn't there. "B has been gone for over a year. I haven't been dating or even looking. She just, fell into my life."

Shyne and Bryonna had been friends since grade school. She was so devastated by the accident that took her friend's life that she wanted to burn down the entire prison just to get to the man. Luckily for the other inmates, her husband Asad was able to talk her down. Sun got revenge on his wife's killer and met Justice the same night. A win/win he took as a sign.

"Yeah well ion got nothing to do with nothing," Killa said and wiped his hands to prove it. He may still be the most dangerous man on the planet but no one wants smoke with Shyne.

"I'll handle Shyne," his mother assured them both. If anyone could it would be her since they were two peas in a pod. "When can we meet her?"

"It's still new but she's the one. There's something about

2

Justice. Like, she's one of us?" Sun tried to explain although it was still new. So new he had yet to even call her since they met in New Orleans a few days ago. He planned to as soon as he hit New York but wanted his parents blessing. At least his mother's since his father seemed shook.

"Come on inside and tell me all about this Justice," Yolo insisted and took her son by his arm.

CHAPTER 1

"Not guilty!" the guilty man repeated when the jury returned their verdict of acquittal. His trial was anything but fair since he paid off, threatened and killed all the witnesses. Things the state usually does and gets away with.

Devil Jones had did a drive-by shooting on his enemy and shot everyone but his intended target. Including the seven year girl who died on the Harlem sidewalk. A hundred people saw the brazen daylight attack but none of them showed up to trial and he was about to walk.

"Pipe down in my courtroom!" the judge boomed and banged his gavel. He looked over at the jury and shook his head. One had a head full of expensive weave and another wore bright diamonds in his ears. Even the jury foreman sported a Rolex and new suit straight out of JC Penny catalog at the start of the trial.

"Whatever you say yo honor!" Devil laughed and ditty bopped out of the court room. He lifted his nose above the child's grieving family on his way out. His nose was so high he didn't even notice the snarls on the angry faces. Especially one, her, the one who would do something about this injustice.

"We waited a year for justice! And what did we get?" the dead child's mother moaned towards the judge. He could only hang his head in reply. He planned to knock the defendant's socks off when he got convicted but the paid for jury set him free. "We want justice!"

"And justice you shall get," Justice mumbled as she left the courtroom. The elevator had just dinged open and she rushed on with Devil and his two co-defendants.

"Them folks tried me! Don't they know the Devil always wins!" Devil laughed as they descended. Everyone laughed along with him except the old lady staring at him. "What's wrong with you old lady?"

"Me?" Justice asked from under the disguise. The old lady getup allowed her to get weapons inside the court. She beeped coming through the metal detector but the guard turned his head and let her keep her knitting needles. She gripped them inside her old lady bag, under the roll of yarn as she scanned the occupants of the elevator. Especially their eyes and necks. She could easily blind and kill them all before they reached the ground floor. Almost did too until her own self warned. "I'll get caught tho."

"Grandma lost her mind!" one of his cronies offered and waited to see if Devil would laugh before he could laugh at his own joke. He did so he cracked up as well.

"See you guys later," Justice said sweetly as the doors opened. The thugs were a lot of things but gentlemen wasn't any of them so they pushed past the old lady and exited the building.

Justice didn't mind since she preferred to be behind them

anyway. They gibbed and gabbed all the way out of the building and over to the parking lot. She followed them all the way back uptown until they reached their block. It was a festive summer day with kids playing Skelly, girls jumping double dutch and old folks enjoying the shade from the buildings. It all came to a screeching halt the moment their custom SUV pulled onto the block.

"The Devil is coming!" a terrified child screamed and pressed the pause button on the entire block. Even the Mr. Softy truck stopped singing it's happy tune and chirped out away from the curb. After a split second pause all out panic ensued and the people all ran for their lives. The jump rope was still in rotation as the girls took off.

"That's right roaches! Scatter! Run!" Devil laughed at the chaos he caused. Never mind that the grandmother who raised him was one of the old people trying to get away. She wasn't moving fast enough so he gave her a little kick to her backside to get her going. "You too granny!"

"This dude is wicked," Justice remarked and shook her head. She had enough ammo to body them all but needed help and knew just who to call.

❄

"Something on your mind Just?" Aunt Viola asked as Justice pushed her famous baked ziti around the plate with her fork.

"Who? Me? Nuh-uh!" she declared and took a huge bite to prove it. Viola and Nuts both shared a 'yeah right' glance since they both know her well enough to know something was on her mind.

"Mmhm," her aunt nodded and resumed eating. Something was eating her but they knew she would get around to it. Both hoped it would be soon since they were still newly-weds and all.

"Yeah, so um, mmhm," Justice hummed and smiled the rest of the way through dinner.

"Her or me?" Nuts finally asked once the plates were clean. It was clear she needed to speak to one of them specif-ically since she had them both and was hemming and hawing instead of speaking.

"You please," she nodded and stood. Viola began to clear the table while they stepped out onto the fire escape. "I like the new place!"

"No!" Nuts said and shook his head vigorously since she always seemed to have a problem understanding that small word.

"No, what? I ain't even said nothing yet?" she reeled and fawned innocently. Not innocently enough because Nuts didn't buy it for a second.

"I watched the Devil trial too. I told Viola you were coming to dinner the second he got off. You called two seconds after that," he explained. He felt the same way about it but if he acted on it, when would it end?

"Nah, I mean, but for real," Justice stuttered and stam-mered in search of the right words. "We gotta give it to him! That poor little girl!"

"I told you, I'm out!" he reiterated, then expounded. "And, this is two person work. So if I'm out, you're out!"

"One last one tho! The devil, who don't wanna kill the devil! Shoot, ask anyone, if you had the chance to kill the devil, shoot, err body wants to kill the devil!" she said, trying to make her case.

"No. Un-uh. Laa. Um, not. Decline..." Nuts insisted in

several languages. He and Justice talked over each other, both trying to get the upper hand. "That's it Justice! It's over! They'll get what's coming to them. The last thing we need is you getting into trouble. Remember Joseph!"

"Yeah, yeah," she sighed and twisted her lips. He definitely saved her butt on her very first mission for justice. Justice let out another sigh and hung her head and slunk back through the living room. Her lips were still twisted when she planted a kiss on her aunt's cheek.

"Good night Justice," Viola sang over her shoulder. Nuts came up behind his wife and planted a kiss on her neck. "I bet I know what that was about?"

"You do?" he asked in semi shock since they kept the business on the hush as much as possible. Viola was a smart lady so she wasn't oblivious to what they did. Just oblivious to the details.

"Yup! About that guy she met down there. She likes him!" she happily declared. They both recalled how giddy Justice was when she came in that night. Especially since she was pouting and moping when she left.

"Yeah, the guy. Mmhm," Nuts agreed. He knew he had some research to do on this Sun person.

Justice of course had already done her research on the intriguing man. Mostly wild rumors and stories about his parents that were too unbelievable to be believed. All she knew was he was 'the he' that she had been waiting for. He was tall, beige, handsome and could throw them hands.

"Wish he was here now," she pouted as she drove home. Each breath Devil and his crew got to breathe insulted her. An insult to the child who died just for jumping rope. "All these killer cops, but they just wanna kill innocent, unarmed black men."

9

Justice was fuming by the time she reached her brownstone. It would have been a great idea to go to bed and sleep it off but she headed down to the basement instead. A plan would have been a good idea too but she was too mad to come up with one.

"You're up papi," she told one of the latex masks staring at her like a creepy audience. Nuts had installed eyes into his latest design as well. Padded male clothes diminished her lady lumps, yet tore away at the seams in case she needed a quick change.

"Eenie, meenie, minie..." she sang as she tried to select a weapon for the night. Some chicks spend an hour picking a purse or pair of shoes while she wondered what caliber went best with her outfit. The good thing about guns is she could carry more than one. "You, and you!"

Justice reached for the corresponding silencers then shook her head. She decided she wanted to make a lot of noise instead. So she could send a lesson along with the lead shower in the forecast. There's always some pawns waiting for the king to die so they can get a seat on the throne. She planned to send that message to them as well.

She was in full character by the time she eased out of the back door and hit the alley. Justice even did a Puerto Rican papi ditty bop a few blocks over to where one of so many cars was parked. She rode over to Queens where a 2021 Escalade waited for its chance.

"Pretty!" she purred at the majestic black, even though it was subject to change. Once she was inside a press of a button pulled up the color control panel. She shook her head and laughed at her own selection. "That's just racist Justice Jackson!"

Loud salsa music boomed through the disco tech worthy

sound system as she pulled away from the curb. The bright pink Cadillac SUV turned heads on every block it turned on. They usually scoped a target before targeting it but she was too heated to be careful.

"Papi must be lost?" one of Devil's men laughed when the Papi-mobile pulled on the block. Even the cops generally didn't pull onto this block without calling first.

"Must be," Devil agreed and stood from the stoop that served as his throne. The truck was too bright and too loud to be a threat so they all looked on curiously. Plus there was only one person in the vehicle. Opps didn't roll like that. They would never bomb without their whole team behind them.

"Good!" Justice said when she saw it was only him, his crew, and a few youngins who needed to see this lesson out on the block. There was a self imposed curfew anytime Devil was at home.

She set the self drive function of the truck and slid over to the passenger seat as she neared. When she got nearer she popped out the passenger window and upped both guns. Devil and his dudes had already stepped out to the curb for a closer look and got a closer look right down the barrel of both guns.

"Oh snap!" Devil declared and turned to run. A quick tug on the trigger from one gun spun him back around. The other gun barked twice and bit chunks out of his chest.

"Oh no you don't!" Justice said but stayed in character when the others tried to run. She fired in each direction and dropped them all. The youngins all ducked for cover but she wasn't after them at the moment. If they decided to fill those dead shoes she just emptied, she had no problem coming back. Unfortunately they weren't the only ones to witness the bright pink Cadillac truck doing a drive by.

"You see that?" a cop exclaimed to his partner as they passed a cross block and saw the Puerto Rican man leaning out with flames spitting from each hand.

"I saw that!" his partner a said and threw the lights and sirens on as he pulled around to catch up.

"Uh-oh! Let's bounce! Oh..." Justice insisted until she remembered no one was behind the wheel. The cops had just pulled on the end of the block when she jumped behind the wheel. They were halfway down when she bent the corner. The half a block lead wasn't enough to getaway unseen.

"There it is!" the passenger cop shouted and pointed at the only Escalade in sight.

"That truck is blue?" the driver asked and scanned the block. He was just as certain the truck they just saw was pink but it was no where to be seen.

"You see another Escalade?" his partner asked. He shrugged his shoulders since he didn't and pulled her over. Both cops drew their weapons and exited the patrol car. They took cover behind the doors and barked orders.

"Let me see your hands!" one cop screamed and tightened his grip on the trigger.

"Don't shoot! I'm white!" Justice pleaded while papi sizzled in the ashtray.

"She is white." the cop on the passenger side confirmed. That led to another dilemma so they moved to save her.

"Come on! We got you!" the first cop screamed and pulled the damsel from her distress. The other snatched open the passenger door and opened fire into the back of the truck.

"Ahhhhh!" he shouted and fired until his gun clicked empty.

"Ayo! Why you shooting up my whip!" Justice fussed out of character but caught herself. "There's no one in there!"

"So, where, did you see, I..." both perplexed police pondered. Once the gun smoke cleared all they saw was broken glass and bullet holes.

"I want your badge numbers! Shooting up a white woman's vehicle! Ought to be ashamed..." she fussed as they slinked back to their patrol car. They did still have an active shooter on the loose which gave them a reason to escape.

"Sorry ma'am, gunman on the loose!" one said over his shoulder as they rushed off.

"Suckers!" Justice snickered and got back into the battered vehicle. She peeled off the mask and headed further uptown to the Bronx. Jerome Avenue was the place cars come to die so it was the perfect place to abandon it. She found a spot, jumped out and quickly walked away with it running.

"Jackpot!" a junkie cheered and high fived his junkie partner. The impact of the hand slap sent them both sprawling on the sidewalk since neither weighed much.

Justice just shook her head at the spectacle as she walked away. Then stopped in her tracks to watch the next spectacle when they hopped inside the truck. The vehicle contained too much of Nut's high tech gadgetry to just leave on the side of the street. As these two junkies were about to find out.

"Son! We gonna get a rock this big!" the driver said, taking his hands off the wheel to demonstrate.

"Bigger!" the other junkie declared hopefully. All hope went out the windows when the whole truck began to sizzle. The self destruct function began to burn the vehicle from the inside out. The junkies waited until the last second before bailing out the ball of fire. All they could do was watch their pipe dreams go up in smoke.

CHAPTER 2

❦

"*J*s it...." Justice wondered when her phone began to ring. She had several phones that rang several times throughout the day. Not this one though, this one was personal. This was the family phone, the one her family used. The number she had given to Sun and she had just gotten off a call with Nuts and Viola. A wide smile spread on her face when she saw the New York number on the screen.

"Yesss!" she cheered, danced and pumped her fist. She was so busy doing her touchdown dance while the phone rang. She was still celebrating when it stopped. "Shoot!"

"Hello? You just called? Who dis?" Justice practiced when she dialed the number back. She ran out of practice time when he picked up.

"Justice?" Sun asked when he took the call. All he got was a goofy giggle before she panicked and hung up. He tilted his head and looked curiously at his phone. He wondered if she had lost interest in the week since they met since he just got to New York. The wondering came to an end when the phone rang again. "Hello?"

"Hey, this is Justice! You called?" she asked happily like Haley. She couldn't quite decide on a character so her old friend from Seal training came to mind.

"This is Sun. We met in the French Quarter?" he had to ask since she didn't sound like he remembered. And he remembered every second of their encounter. Justice grimaced on her end, shook it off and came back as herself.

"You mean kicking butt and taking names in the French quarter!" she corrected and laughed. The ice was broken and they began to talk. A good talk that meant flipping upside down on the sofa with her feet on the wall.

"Was that a yawn?" Sun asked a while later and looked at his watch.

"Well, it is dawn," she reminded, not needing to look at hers. The sun was just peeking above the horizon which meant they talked all night.

"Probably should get some breakfast then huh?" he suggested. Justice's head began nodding before her brain could catch up. Another big yawn put things back into perspective. "Better yet, lunch."

"Lunch sounds good!" she agreed. It took twenty minutes of goodbyes and see you laters before they finally did hang up.

"I got a date! I got a date!" Justice sang and danced all the way to her room. Sleep came easy and dreams were pleasant. She awoke later that afternoon and prepared for her very first date. Easier said than done for someone who had never been on one before.

❄

"*Y*ou look nice!" Justice sang and did a twirl in her full length mirrors. The long evening gown flowed with her and reminded her that it was way too much. "Nice for a debutante ball, not lunch!"

Justice extracted herself from the ball gown and started from scratch. Her next outfit made her look sexy and sophisticated but the business skirt suit was a bit too much for lunch as well. She lost track of time as she hopped in and out of various clothes. The doorbell chimed and confused her even more.

"Who the heck.." she wondered and went over to the monitor to see Sun standing in front of the door. Just the sight of him made her gush and giggle once more. He rang again a minute later and she got herself together enough to lean into the intercom. "One second please!"

"Uh, OK," Sun replied into the speaker.

"Shoot, shoot, shoot!" Justice fussed at her tardiness. Being late was something she never did. It was a sign of weakness in her book. She pulled on a pair of khaki pants, pullover shirt and sneakers.

This was as good an excuse to use the emergency pole as any. It doesn't matter how old, or how many bodies a person drops, when they slide from the third floor to the basement they're going to say, "Weeeeeeee!"

Justice rushed out the back door, down the alley, around the corner and up the fire escape. She unlocked the window with one of Nut's devices and rushed inside the apartment to let Sun in. She was worried about him thinking she was a spoiled rich girl so she had him pick her up from just one of many apartments she kept around the city, state and country.

"Hey!" Justice cheered happily when she opened the door.

Her smile made him forget every one of the ten minutes he had been waiting. Plus, she still wanted to get dressed.

"Hey yourself! You look great!" Sun announced and tossed her thoughts of changing right out the same window she just crawled in.

"You look niiiiiice!" she sang, cackled and got all goofy again. If Sun had a ring in his pocket he might have dropped to one knee and asked her to marry him at that moment. Men know if a woman is his woman within the first two and a half minutes.

"Thanks, you ready?" he asked and extended his arm. Justice looped hers in his and followed him down to the street.

"Nice car!" Justice sang as she admired the shiny new Benz that answered the button press on the key fob.

"Uh, thanks," he said and second guessed using his new car. He wanted to impress her but it could also lead to her asking what he does for a living. He had no idea how she would take his killing bad guys for a living. Bad people usually make good money so he confiscates it. "Nice neighborhood."

"It wasn't always," she sighed and looked in the direction that was once restricted by melanin. Had her dad lived a few years more he wouldn't have had to die. She made sure to turn her head as they neared the brownstone she actually lived in.

"Always wanted one of these brownstones. That one is really nice!" Sun admired in general, then of hers specifically.

"Huh?" she nearly panicked, then relaxed as he scanned the rest of the renovated properties. "Oh, they cool."

Small yet calculated talk bounced around the Benz as they headed uptown. Manhattan's busy streets added action to the soundtrack. Sun wanted to make a good second impression on their first date so he headed to a New York city icon.

"Where are we going!" Justice demanded when she realized where he was taking her.

"Tavern On The Green. That's OK isn't it?" he asked, ready to pull a U-turn if it wasn't.

"Um, yeah? OK, I guess. Sure!" she decided after a short debate. Only Sun would find that attractive but then again, his mother was a lunatic. His father was a goon like his brothers and his sister was Shyne. So, yeah he got it.

Justice relaxed since she couldn't possibly be recognized from her last visit here. That one didn't turn out so well since she beat her date to death with a bottle before jumping over the rail and outrunning the police on a horse drawn buggy.

"I won't hit you in your pretty head," Justice thought as they walked towards the eatery. Or, at least she thought it was internal.

"I appreciate that," Sun said and patted his pocket to make sure he didn't have a ring anywhere.

"Right this way," a pretty waitress sang flirtatiously. Justice snarled at her smiling at her date but Sun looked everywhere else but her. He had been married before so he was a pro at lowering his gaze. When he lifted it again it landed on Justice.

"Not this table!" she fussed when she returned to the scene of the crime. It was no longer a crime scene but she wouldn't mind sitting at a different table.

"I'm sorry sir, there are no other tables," the waitress pleaded to Sun.

"But, I'm the one speaking to you," Justice reminded sweetly. Still, Sun saw a flash of crazy in her and liked it.

"We can go somewhere else if..." he offered but she shook it off.

"No, this is fine," Justice sang and sat. The waitress look at her for the first time and nodded.

"I know dear. Every since that crazy girl beat that man to death people have been avoiding this table," she confided. Then added, "Then again, some people request it!"

"Oh yeah! How could I forget!" Sun laughed. The sun caught his eyes just right and now Justice almost asked for his hand in marriage. "That was crazy yo!"

"I have the video!" the waitress conspired and pulled her phone from her apron. She leaned in to offer her cleavage along with the video but he was only interested on the woman with the bottle.

"She's a beast!" Sun said in awe. Justice was just about to snatch the phone out of her hand and throw it as far as she could into the park. His next words just d the waitress her thousand dollar phone. "I love her!"

"Love you too," she mumbled but both Sun and the waitress turned their heads. "Would love some lemonade too! Y'all have lemonade? I just love me some lemonade! Mmhm, yup."

"Sure! What else can I get you?" the waitress asked once she remembered being a waitress. Sun ordered for them both and earned a few more cool points for being a good listener. They had talked about favorite foods and colors so he ordered what she liked.

The happy couple ordered and ate while getting to know each other better. Nothing was written down or nothing but both knew they were a couple by the time their dessert saucers were clean. Neither wanted to leave yet but the next couple with reservation had arrived. They stepped back out and looked around for a reason to delay the inevitable departure.

"Ever rode one of those?" Sun asked as a empty carriage came near.

"Um..." she wondered since technically she had when she killed Gwap and made her getaway. "You mean like, inside? No, un-uh."

"Um, OK. Let's take a ride," he suggested even though he wasn't crazy about horses. He was crazy about the woman with him though and wasn't ready to leave her.

"Sure!" Justice cheered and he raised his hand to hail the driver.

"Off duty," the man said, shaking his head. Sun wasn't the type who took no for and answer so he dug into his pocket and came up with a better answer. President Ben Franklin's face has been turning 'no' into 'yes' since it was first printed. "Like I was saying, welcome aboard."

Justice was impressed and allowed him to help her up into the carriage. She cuddled up next to him and rested her head on his shoulder as they pulled away. Some of the best conversations are had without saying a words. This was one of them as they watched the park and people pass by.

"Yes!" Justice decided emphatically and popped up.

"Yes what?" Sun asked since neither had said a word since climbing aboard.

"Huh? Oh, naw, cuz I was like, mmhm," she stammered, embarrassed since the proposal she heard was only in her head. That or she could read his mind.

The carriage ride ended but the ride back to Brooklyn was quieter. Both were quite in their feelings about their lunch date coming to an end even if it was now dinner time.

They both let out a love sick sigh when he pulled to the building where he picked her up.

"Ion even live here," Justice blurted when he turned the car off. "But you can walk me. If you want?"

"I want," he agreed and took her hand. Justice tried to keep her composure but a goofy laugh bubbled to the surface. The last time she walked hand in hand with a man she was six and that man was her father.

"Here," she announced and sighed when they reached the brownstone.

"Word," Sun nodded and laughed. It didn't dawn on him that she owned the whole building when she used her key to open the door. He didn't expect a kiss so he extended a hand. "So..."

"Yes!" she agreed to whatever he was asking. "Dinner, breakfast, lunch, a snack!"

"I want all that. I'll call you tomorrow," Sun said and changed his mind about the kiss. He planted one on her cheek and sent her into another giggle fit. She tripped over her threshold and fell in her foyer as Sun walked away.

He didn't get far before he sensed danger. Brooklyn could be dangerous in general but this was a familiar danger he knew well. He quickly scanned the area and saw danger headed right for him.

"Mmhm!" Shyne hummed maniacally.

"Are you following me?" he asked incredibly.

"You mean to Tavern On The Green, and horse and buggy rides? Nope, un-uh," she denied and glared over at Justice's building.

"Bruh, leave her alone!" Sun warned sternly.

"I should say the same to you!" Shyne pouted. "B still warm in her grave and you out here with some chick!"

"First of all, my wife died a year ago. I wasn't even thinking about anyone new. The kids are with her mom. I'm alone. I'm lonely," Sun sighed. It was touching and true but Shyne wasn't moved.

"Ain't nobody never died from being lonely," Shyne retorted and crossed her arms. "She cute tho. Unless I bite her nose off."

"She's different, special," he said softly and his twin softened. Shyne knew she had to be something since he told their parents about her. That's how she found out from their baby sister.

"Well, she better be. Cuz I want all the smoke..." Shyne said over her shoulder as she walked off. "All, the smoke ..."

"Save that smoke for later!" He reminded since they were in the city for a reason.

CHAPTER 3

"Donnel MacArthur. Age thirty seven, no six. Thirty six, his birthday is in two days," Sun briefed his sister on their target. They made good money running the 1-800-Killa line as well as freelancing but this was some pro bono work because some people just needed dead. He presided on the jury that just set a killer free for a fee.

"Thirty six it is because he's not getting a day older," Shyne growled as she studied the before and after pictures of their target. He was looking a lot better after the trial than before since Devil Jones had paid him and several other jurors off.

Devil was at the top of their list but someone had beaten them to him and murdered the whole crew. That seemed to happen more and more as of late but justice is justice so it didn't really matter. Dead is dead and that was all that really mattered.

"Next on the list, Deborah Dixon," Sun said and pulled up her social media. Her before and afters were a lot easier since she was Raggedy Ann at the start of the trial and Cardi B before the verdict was announced. Devil broke good bread for his freedom but she ran through it in a week. Broke people are so used to being broke they will spend whatever they get as soon as possible so they can be broke again.

"The lawyer too! He was down with it!" Shyne reminded since the biased barrister facilitated the payoffs. He too was pushing a new Porsche once his client got off.

"Him too. Let's get this done so you can get back to Asad and the kids," Sun offered sweetly but his sister saw straight through it like glass.

"You mean so you can get back to your little girlfriend!" she huffed and poked her lip out. She was really cool with it by now since she knew he was happy. All that matters was her family being happy.

"That too. I'm thinking about taking her to meet mom and dad?" he asked as he steered towards their first target. He just so happened to map the hits out leading to JFK airport. The sooner his lunatic sister was gone the better.

"Wow," Shyne sighed and accepted this was serious. They both mulled on it all the way to Polo Grounds where Donnel MacArthur used to live since they were about to put him in the past tense.

Research had him hitting a local bar to take swats at the local barflies. Sometimes he caught one, other times he didn't. Either way he would be sloppy drunk by the end of the night. It looked like this was a good night when they spotted their target walking out of the bar. He was arm in arm with a lady of the night smiling from ear to ear.

"I'll be right back," Shyne said when the couple dipped into an alley to handle a transaction.

"Chill. Don't traumatize the woman for nothing," Sun

warned to her back. He didn't like killing people in front of other people if it could be avoided.

"She looks like she's already traumatized if you ask me," Shyne huffed and turned her nose up at the white woman in the tiny dress. She had a grudge against prostitutes but it wasn't publishable by death most times. Sometimes it was when a knowingly sick person knowingly spreads their sickness. In that case, they too needed dead and she had no problem giving them dead.

"Mmhm," Sun hummed at the black woman's booty bouncing around in the dress. They both kept an eye on the entire alley so they could catch Donnel when he came out. A familiar flash lit up for a split second but it wasn't accompanied by the usual bang. "What the..."

Sun may have wondered but Shyne hopped out to go see for herself. Half a step later her brother was half a step in front of her. Both had guns at their sides and both upped them when they reached the alley. They blinked at the sight of Donnel stretched out behind the dumpster. The hole in his head explained why as well as the flash. His eyes were still wide from the shock of the sudden death.

"A silencer?" Sun asked rhetorically since he knew. The real question was why a hooker would have one. Shyne had an even better question as she scanned the empty alley.

"Where did she go?" she wondered and looked up at the buildings surrounding her. "Who was that, Spider-Man?"

"Yeah, where?" he agreed and turned to leave. This was now a crime scene and that's no place to be seen. They made haste back to the car and crossed the name off their list.

"The lawyer lives over the bridge," Shyne said once they pulled away from the scene.

"Yeah," Sun agreed since he had set it up in this order

anyway. Justice had some business to attend so they had a late date for ice cream.

Shyne had tapped into his Wi-Fi and got his itinerary. He had ordered a massage from a local oriental parlor. The delivery was free but the happy ending was extra. She pulled a wig on her head and shades on her face to disguise her identity. Nowhere as sophisticated as the disguises made by Nuts but it got the job done.

"Yo, no speeches, no dramatics. Just off him and let's go," Sun warned when they arrived. Shyne responded by checking the back seat, under her seat and in the glove box. "What are you looking for?"

"Not what, who," she said and checked the back seat once again. "Looking for who you telling what to do."

"Ha, ha. Handle your business. The next one is mine," he said as she got out. He could only shake his head to her happily skipping into the building. Shyne noticed a tall Asian woman exit the elevator as she neared. They both ignored each other while taking note of each other in passing.

"At least he'll be nice and relaxed," Shyne mused to herself and pressed the button for the lawyer's floor. She pulled the tools for her trade as she rode up to the penthouse on the elevator. The smell from the Asian woman's perfume still hovered in the air.

"Bad girls move in silence and violence..." Shyne sang in a whisper as she made it down the hall. She kept her head down to avoid the cameras and reached his door. It was slightly ajar and she was fully alert as she crept inside. The sound of a running shower guided her like a GPS system.

Shyne expected to see the man standing in the shower but found him stretched out instead. A neat hole in his temple explained the why, now she needed the who. She whipped the gun in each direction and eased back out of the bedroom. The same perfume hung in the air and she knew the perpetrator was long gone.

"That was quick?" Sun said when his sister returned to the car. The perplexed look on her face made him ask, "What?"

"He's dead!" she replied and looked around for the Asian woman she knew was long gone.

"Duh, you're Shyne. Of course he's dead!" Sun reminded.

"Yeah I am but, I didn't kill him?" she sighed since he had been hit exactly how she would have hit him. One in the dome and go home. Bullet to the temple, nice and simple.

"What the... Let's go!" Sun declared and chirped away from the curb. Deborah Dixon lived over in Queens near the airport so he saved her for last. Now he raced over to get there before someone else could. They weren't going to make it. They had been beaten to a kill from time to time but this was two in one night. Not including Devil and his crew.

"Yooooo!" Shyne exclaimed when they reached their destination and found a full blown crime scene. They found a place to park and mixed in with the crowd of gawkers. "What happened?"

"Ole Deborah got kilt! Knew that was gonna happen. All that fronting lately! New hair, shoes, nails..." a woman went on and on. She hissed like a real hater as she poured the dead woman's business out.

"Next of kin? Any family out here?" a detective asked as he came out.

"I'm her sister!" the same woman who was just hating on her called out. She raised her hand and was escorted under the police tape.

"Welp, let's get you to the airport!" Sun shrugged. The sooner he got rid of her, the sooner he could see his Justice.

"Or, I can just hang out with my big brother!" she suggested and took his hand.

"Or not," he laughed and pulled away. Shyne let out her sinister cackle as he sped off to the airport. "No time to stop. I'll slow down so you can jump out. Tuck and roll."

"I'll tuck and roll you!" she threatened. He wasn't exactly sure what that meant but didn't want to find out either. He pulled up to the departure section and made a complete stop.

"Happy?" he asked and leaned over to pull the handle.

"No, but I will be," she said with a smirk. "See you later."

"Mmhm, not if I see you first," Sun mumbled to himself as he pulled off. He texted Justice as he merged into traffic.

"Un-huh! Un-huh!" Justice danced when the text came through. She was so busy dancing she almost forgot to reply. "Oh yeah!"

"Un-huh!" Sun cheered when he got her reply. He entered the address to the ice cream shop into the GPS and followed it back over to Brooklyn.

Red Hook was once a down and dirty, dangerous hood but now it's all good. Trap houses and shooting galleries were replaced by sushi spots and art galleries. Plus a gourmet ice cream parlor Sun found to show off. It wasn't necessarily necessary since Justice was wide open. Sun parked and entered the nostalgic eatery and found Justice seated at the bar wide eyed, with a wide smile.

'Don't get all goofy again' Justice demanded to herself as he came near. It was a stern warning but she felt herself getting goofier with each step. She was a full blown goofball by the time he arrived.

"Hey you. Are you OK ?" Sun wondered when she swooned like she might pass out. Chicks had that same reaction to him since he inherited his famous father's swag at sixteen.

"I am beautiful ! No, you are. You are beautiful !" she stammered, trying to get it right. She had practiced a sultry greeting and pose in the mirror but it flew out one of the open windows when Sun came through the door.

"No, you are," he corrected and sent her into a giggle fit. "Let's get a table, and order?"

"OK," she agreed and followed him over to an empty table. "Can I have Rocky road?"

"You can literally have whatever you want," Sun said into her eyes and int o to her soul. "I'll have the same."

"Make it three," a voice said over the sound of a chair sliding up to the table. Both turned their heads to the interloper.

"Uh..." Justice said and began to stand so she could fight the chick bold enough to crash her date. She noticed the family facial structure before she could and kept standing so she could introduce herself properly. "You must be Shyne!"

"I..." Shyne was saying something slick but Justice pulled her into a hug before she could get it out. The warm hug melted her cold heart a little and rendered the smart comment moot. Shyne smiled at her brother telling her about her.

Sun watched in relief since it was going better than expected. He did notice when his sister scrunched her face as if Justice stunk. The expensive perfume she wore actually smelled wonderful. It was something and whatever it was, she would tell him.

"So, three Rocky Roads it is!" Sun said and didn't get another word in for the rest of the night. Shyne and Justice chopped it up like he wasn't even there. Until the bill came and they both turned towards him.

"No, let me!" he teased and paid the bill.

"It was so nice meeting you!" Shyne cheered when they stepped out of the restaurant.

"Likewise! We must hook up again!" Justice replied.

"Oh! Our parents are having a cookout next weekend in Atlanta. You have to come!" Shyne insisted.

"Yeah I was..." Sun tried to interject but it was girl time. He planned to invite her to the cookout himself but didn't get a chance to speak since his sister came.

"I would love to!" Justice agreed. Sun got her to herself for a minute when he walked her to her car.

"I'll send your tickets tomorrow," he sighed, almost nervously.

"Meet the parents, wow!" she said when it hit her. She didn't have formal parents anymore but Aunt Viola and Nuts would fit the bill. Sun nodded, smiled, then planted a kiss on her cheek. He waited until she pulled away before turning back to his sister.

"What kinda kiss was that?" Shyne teased, even though she pegged Justice as a good girl.

"Are you cra..." he started to ask, but already knew the answer. Shyne was the textbook definition of crazy so he moved on to his next question. "What was that look? When y'all hugged?"

"This may sound crazy but she's one of us!" she declared, then explained. " Her perfume. It was at the building in Jersey! The tall Asian lady!"

"Bruh, have you lost your, never mind," Sun said and abandoned that question too since he was sure Shyne had long ago lost her mind. "No way! She's a, a... You think?"

CHAPTER 4

"OK then!" Justice sang as she stepped out to the waiting limo. She was a billionaire herself but rarely treated herself to the luxuries that came with it. She had gotten used to flying private though so she was happy when the car arrived at the private section of the airport. She was even happier when she boarded and found Sun aboard.

"Hey you," he greeted and stood for a hug.

"Thought you had business?" she asked before the embrace that made her knees buckle.

"You are my business," he said into her eyes. Justice blushed and pulled away. "You OK?"

"Huh? Yeah!" she insisted. She wasn't, but no way was she about to admit to him that he made her feel tingly all over. The talk was vibrant and playful during the flight, until the pilot announced their descent in Atlanta. Then took a more serious tone.

"Look, my family is crazy," he admitted. "All of them. My mom, dad. Shyne, the little ones. Even grandma Diedra . She ain't got it all either."

"So, how'd you manage to stay sane?" she wondered and tilted her head.

"Huh?" Sun answered since he didn't have an answer to that one. In fact, he dipped inside his head and looked around for the answer. All he found in there was a bunch of crazy. But crazy is like cholesterol, some good, some bad. The Killa clan was good crazy.

"Don't worry. I'll be fine," she said when they reached the car Sun kept at the airport. It just happened to be one aisle over from the one she kept. The friendly talk resumed all the way out to the house.

❄

"Search those two," Yolo warned her husband while she fussed over the food. She had come a long way from cooking babies over the years. Now she cooked, baked and knitted her days away.

"Un-uh! Come here girl!" Killa fussed when his young daughter tried to make a run for it.

"Yes father?" little Diedra asked and batted her eyes up at her darling daddy. It usually worked but he had his orders and his boss was standing there watching.

"Hands on the wall. You too!" he ordered. This wasn't the first time the kids had been frisked so they knew the position and assumed it. Killa started with her since she tried to make a run. He shook his head when he found a set of brass knuckles on her.

"OK daddy!" the child cheered and tried to walk off.

"Oh no you don't!" he said and finished frisking her. The search turned up another set of brass knuckles, nunchucks and a slingshot. "And what do you have boy?"

"Just this," little Killa sighed and came off his own nunchucks. Then some Chinese throwing stars, a butterfly knife and other assorted weapons.

"Just this huh," Killa said as he disarmed his son. The kids skipped off happily while he turned to his wife. "I'm worried about those two."

"Yeah, you should be. We have bail money tho," Yolo shrugged and went back to her meal.

"They're here!" Grandma Diedra called from her rocking chair on the porch.

"Should have searched her too," Killa mumbled as the family all stepped outside to meet Sun's new friend. Her being here meant something in itself so they would be on their best behavior.

Justice tensed when she saw the Forrest family gathered on the front porch to meet her. She tried to place names to faces as Sun pulled to a stop behind the family minivan. No one looked anything like the murky reports floating around the internet. She now doubted the whole Killa/Yolo folklore.

Killa looked like any other suburban dad with a polo shirt with a round pouch in the middle. He wore hippie sandals and no socks instead of the wheat Timberlands his image suggested he wore. Yolo was a pretty suburban housewife, with her natural hair pulled into a bun and apron over her sundress. The old lady looked to be the most dangerous of the bunch with her discriminatory stare.

"You ready?" Sun asked as he put the car in reverse in case she wasn't.

"Ready!" Sh shot back and opened her own door. Grandma Diedra nodded in approval at the move. She was a bougie as it gets but still opened her own doors.

"Hey guys, meet Justice!" Sun greeted and watched as she

gracefully met the closest people on the planet to him. Justice beamed brightly and extended her hand to grandma first.

"How many kids you got?" Diedra wanted to know before accepting her hand.

"I've never been married ma'am," Justice explained and got another nod of approval. She was looking for a number but liked that answer even better. She shook all hands and smiled in all faces as Sun named the family.

"Well, come with me dear," Yolo directed and took her into the kitchen with the womenfolk while the men retreated to the deck. "You too young lady!"

"Huh? Who?" little Diedra wanted to know. She would much rather go with the guys but Yolo wouldn't hear of it. The women didn't do enough cursing and spitting for her taste.

Shyne and company arrived soon and it was a full house. Justice harbored mixed emotions as they all mixed and mingled around the large dinner table. This was family, something she got cheated out of by the mean streets and crooked cops. She wasn't sure if she should laugh or cry.

"You gonna marry my brother?" Diedra dared out of the blue. The three distinct conversations around the table all came to a screeching halt.

"Girl, stay out grown folks business!" Yolo chided from her end of the table. It sounded good but she still looked over to their guest to see how she would answer.

"I wanna hear this!" grandma proclaimed and leaned in. All eyes beamed in on Justice to see if she would fold under the pressure.

"Y'all do know, we just met a couple weeks ago!" Sun butted in and reached for the bread. "Y'all gonna scare her off!"

"It's ok, I don't scare easily," Justice replied. The warm smile belied the improvised explosive devices and snipers she encountered in Iraq. Shootouts, car chases and fist fights she had been in. She looked directly at the nosey little girl and explained, "I am definitely going to marry your brother."

"OK then!" Shyne cheered and high fived her. The banter quickly filled the large dining room once again. Justice had unofficially joined the world's most dangerous family. Even if she still didn't believe a word of what she read online. They were a typical, upper middle class black family as far as she could see. Killa and Yolo were Cliff and Claire Huxtable as far as she could tell.

"Well, you young people have fun. We're going to turn in," Killa announced after dessert. Old people don't last long after a good meal and strawberry shortcake.

"Good night! Nice meeting you!" Justice sang and hugged them both before they retired for the evening. They were going to turn in alright. Turn into the most dangerous couple on the face of the earth.

"You can sleep in my room!" little Diedra offered and took Justice by the hand. She would have too if grandma hadn't intervened.

"She has the guest room," the old lady said and took her other hand. "Make sure ain't no late night creeping around here..."

❄

"*L*et's ride!" Killa announced once they reached their spacious master bedroom.

"Let's!" Yolo cheered and pulled her dress off.

Killa got stuck watching her as she slipped into some comfortable killing clothes.

A dangerous new politician was making a lot of noise as he rose up the ranks. Alfred White was a young, charismatic bigot who was on the fast track to become the next president. The world couldn't stand another Trump-type in office so they planned to make sure he didn't live long enough to get there. Donald Trump had recently died in his sleep and he was a shoe in to replace him.

Once they were dressed to kill they eased out the French doors and into the garage. An app on the phone slid the minivan to the side and gave access to a staircase. Killa was usually a gentleman but shoved his wife aside and ran down the steps first. He called himself beating her to their latest addition but Yolo had struck first.

"Mmhm!" she laughed when he found the empty spot on the wall where the new K/Y 2000 once hung. It was an updated version of the infamous DC/2000. The new device was streamlined and shot a thin coil of steel string. Once it wrapped around the target's neck it would contract until the head popped off. The Killa/Yolo 2000 was deadly efficient.

"Awe man!" he pouted and settled for a pair of fully automatic pistols and extended clips. More than enough for the ragtag country boys

"Looks like he has his proud boys with him!" Yolo sang merrily since the more dead bigots the merrier.

"Proud girls!" Killa corrected and grabbed the seldom used EMS-2000. Short for the emasculator since it was designed to snatch off private parts. It was Shyne's idea but it got shelved since her parents felt it was too extreme. Not as extreme as the violent hatred against whole races of people so it got pulled off the shelf. "We may as well swing down the Old town road while we're out?"

"Yeah, finish the job," Yolo laughed when she got the joke. She grabbed her favorite sniper rifle from the rack and led the way back upstairs. Once upon a time they drove specialized vehicles to make crime scenes but these days the minivan worked just as well.

Killa used the same app to conceal the steps to their arsenal, then open the stash spots in the minivan. He loaded the weapons inside while Yolo loaded her pretty self into the passenger seat. Killa got behind the wheel and pulled away from the house.

"Turn in?" Justice wondered to herself as she watched the van back out of the driveway. A deep sigh escaped her chest since she wished she could ease away and handle some business of her own. Alfred White and his hillbilly proud boys were in town. They were on her radar too and she had planned to derail his political ambitions the first chance she got.

※

"*Y*eeeee-haaaaaw!" Cleotis screamed for no reason except that's what hillbillies do. He was the captain of the proud boys so it was his responsibility to make the rebel call from time to time.

"Yeah, no, are you going to keep doing that?" Alfred White asked. Truth be told the New Jersey raised racist had no love for the hillbillies who supported him. Just like Trump loathed the rednecks who loved him. His was a privileged white people's racism while the country boys' hatred was born from watching as other people from other races pass them in everything. He played up to those same hillbillies and rednecks since they would put him in office.

Or not, since some killers had just pulled up to the rented mansion he was staying in while in Atlanta. Little did he know Yolo had tapped into his assistant's itinerary to book the stay. The house backed up to the wooded area where they would start their attack. Yolo screwed a foot long silencer to the tip of the sniper rifle and got out.

"One, two, three, four dead rednecks!" she counted like the Count from Sesame Street. Once she located the guards posted outside she methodically mowed them down. "OK, bye!"

"Got 'em ?" Killa asked purely rhetorically since she didn't miss. Still, he couldn't hear the *pst, pst, pst, pst,* of the silenced rifled that dropped the guards like dominoes.

"I got 'em!" She cheered. The scope had a camera so they could watch the footage of it later. Nothing is as entertaining as watching people get what they deserve.

"Hope you saved me some," he mumbled as they drove around to the front of the house. They had been gaining access to victims the same way for decades so there was no reason to stop now. He rolled right up to the gate and rang the bell.

"Some niggers at the gate? Anyone ordered some niggers?" Alfred laughed as he looked at them through the security camera. The rednecks inside all laughed along with him but the ones outside didn't find it too funny. Dead people can't take a joke.

"Pizza!" Killa announced and gave his best sambo smile. Bigots love a smiling negro, that's why sellouts are always smiling.

"Let him in boys!" the chief of security radioed to the men outside. Except their radios don't reach into the afterlife so they missed it. "Dang meth monsters! I'll get it..."

The chief stepped out to get it and got it. A silent slug to his forehead sent him with his friends and allowed the killer couple entry to the house. They followed their ears and found Alfred and the others watching movies in the den.

"Someone ordered nigga pie?" Killa greeted in his black sambo voice as they stepped in the room. Their presence and the presence of the guns in their hands froze the men in their places.

"Ooh I was gonna use that line! My favorite part of the movie!" Yolo gushed. "How much to make whites only pie, into a nigga pie?"

"I liked Hoppin Bob! Tell them 'bout the gun line Bob!" Killa recalled and cracked up. They would have gone on reliving lines from the movie Life but got rudely interrupted.

"What's the meaning of this!" Alfred demanded and stood. His white privilege made guns disappear in his mind. The so-called proud boys didn't grow up with any spoon in their mouths especially not the silver spoon Alfred had but still stood with him.

"How's this thing work?" Killa asked his wife, ignoring the man. Alfred was still complaining while they tried to remember how to operate the Emasculator.

"Aim, and pull this..." Yolo said and pulled the lever that sent a miniature bear trap at one of the proud boy's genitals. It was attached to a chain connected to the device.

"Yeeeoooooowww!" the man screeched as it bit into his manhood. His high pitched scream nearly shattered windows and eardrums.

"I bet," Killa grimaced like every man in the room.

"This the good part!" Yolo cheered since she couldn't relate. She hit the same lever and retracted the chain, snatching his package away. "And just like that, a proud girl!"

"Forget this!" one of the other men said and went for his gun. Killa gave him a fighting chance and let him grab it. To his surprise the man put it to his own temple and fired.

"I heard that," Killa laughed. He couldn't blame him for wanting to die as a man instead of a woman like his friend bleeding out on the floor. Yolo quickly shot the rest down with conventional guns and left Alfred the last man standing.

"You want my wallet? Take it. Buy all the cracks, malt liquor, weave and whatever you people like!" he shouted and tossed it towards their feet. That's where it landed and where it would stay since they weren't here for his money.

"Let me show you how to use it..." Yolo offered and reached for their latest toy of their trade. Killa began to hand it over before catching on.

"Oh no you don't! You're getting all the kills. This one is mine!" he fussed. He was right but she denied it. They went back and forth while Alfred tried to ease away. A smile eased into the corner of his mouth when he reached the threshold. Only because he didn't see Killa raising the latest addition to their arsenal. He fired at the same moment Alfred's brain sent the 'run' command to his legs.

The coils found its mark just as he took off. He made two good strides before it snapped shut and lopped his head off. The head rolled one way while the body kept on running. He was headed headless towards the stairs but a body really does need a head to navigate a staircase. The killer couple snickered as the headless body bounced down the flight of steps and landed at the bottom.

"This K/Y jelly thing works good!" Killa nodded.

"K/Y 2000 silly!" his wife corrected and shook her head. Their work was done so they headed back out to the burbs and into the bedroom. It would be an early day since they had company.

CHAPTER 5

"Good morning Miss Diedra!" Justice chimed when she found Grandma Diedra alone in the kitchen. Both shared the habit of waking up before the rest of the world just so they could have an advantage. The person who wakes up at nine will never catch up with the person who wakes up at five.

"That's Grandma Diedra to you, young lady!" she fussed playfully and poured Justice a cup of coffee. They retreated to the back deck to make small talk while the sun rose. By the time it did they were best of friends.

"OK then! If you're looking for cool points, that's where they are!" Yolo announced when she found her son's new boo cooking a big breakfast with Diedra.

"She cool with me! That's all that counts!" Diedra snapped back.

"With me too," Sun said as he came into the kitchen. He was trying to be sweet but still got chased off by his grandmother. "So, I'll just be in the dining room with the guys.

"Mmhm," his mother hummed since he knew better, then turned to their house guest. "Did you sleep well?"

"Oh my God, did I!" she cheered. The long night of traveling the tristate area conducting a triple homicide had taken its toll on her.

"That's great!" Yolo agreed since she had a busy night herself. Justice remembered her and her husband slipping out last night and asked.

"Sleep well?" she asked casually while fixing a plate for Sun.

"Like a rock! My husband and I were out as soon as we hit the room! Old people!" she laughed but not as hard as Grandma Diedra.

"Child who's plate is that supposed to be?" she cackled at the regular size portion on the plate. Even little Killa ate more than that.

"You never fixed a man's plate before?" Yolo reeled in shock. Not that she had before hooking up with her husband and getting domesticated herself.

"My dad, a long time ago," she answered and twisted her lips to prevent herself from crying. Yolo and Diedra saw her reaction and quickly steered the conversation in another direction.

"The Forest men eat!" Yolo proudly proclaimed. She meant it a couple different ways but the other half of the double entendre went right over her head.

"Shole do!" Grandma Diedra cosigned and high-fived Yolo. She was married to a Forest man herself once upon a time. But, that's another story like Hadiyah always says.

"Oh my!" Justice reeled as the women piled food high on the plates. Even little Killa's had more food than she could possibly eat.

"Hey guys!" Shyne sang as she rushed into the kitchen and over to the TV in the fridge. "Check it!"

'Controversial presidential candidate Alfred White was murdered last night along with eight of his security detail...'

"Did you bring juice?" was all Yolo wanted to know.

"I did. Got that nasty stuff daddy drinks too!" Shyne said with a grimace as she produced a bottle of prune juice.

"Whatever. Your father gets cranky if he can't get a good bm," Yolo explained. It was all so interesting but not as interesting as the major news story they acted like they didn't hear a minute ago. That was a big deal but they brushed it off to talk about juice and bowel movements.

"Totally, too much info!" Shyne grimaced and shook her head.

"Wait a minute...." Justice thought as two and two merged in her mind. The reports of this killer family could really be true since she was sure she saw them leave the house last night. Even though Yolo claimed to have gone straight to sleep. It swirled around in her head until she noticed all eyes on her.

"What's wrong baby?" Diedra asked.

"Huh?" Justice wondered.

"You just said, wait a minute?" Yolo reminded.

"Oh yeah. Mmhm," she nodded and turned back to the plates.

"Yeah she's one of us!" Shyne cheered at the slight display of crazy. "Grab those plates so we can feed our men!"

"So, what are you guys doing today? While us girls have some girl time." Yolo directed to her first born.

Sun just blinked to process the prospect of Justice going anywhere with his mother, grandmother and sister. They had been on their best behavior but they usually were at home. But you can't take them anywhere, just like Sun and Shyne when they were young.

"Oh she'll be fine!" Diedra fussed across the table.

"Yeah I do need your help with that thing today son," Killa told Sun.

"Thought that was done?" Sun asked since he knew his parents paid the bigots a visit last night.

"Our work is never done," his father reminded. He was right too because there was always someone somewhere in need of dead.

"It isn't," he agreed and nodded. 1-800-Killa was now government sanctioned and financed. They got the dirty jobs the police were too dirty to do. Not to mention their own freelance work to take out the garbage.

"Well, get cute girls. Since I already am," Shyne laughed. The woman all stood from the now cluttered table and walked off.

"No, we'll get this!" Killa called after them. Not that he minded since being in service to family is the definition of manhood. Sun sighed but he was a man too so he stood and began to clear the table. Asad did his part as well and loaded the dishwasher.

"Ma please..." Sun pleaded when the woman appeared once more. They were all cute in sundresses and sandals but cute has never prevented the Forest women from mayhem.

"Boy stop," she laughed and led the ladies out of the house.

"Granny!" Shyne shrieked when she saw a little too much movement in her grandmother's dress. Are you wearing a thong?"

"We called them g-strings in my day and yes!" the old lady said and flipped her hair. Yolo just laughed and pressed the remote to open the garage. The minivan was fine for family outings but they were all too cute for it today. Today Yolo dropped the top on the Bentley and they piled in.

"Let's do a little shopping!" Diedra suggested since chicks like shopping no matter how old they get.

"West End Mall!" Shyne cheered with a little too enthusiasm. Justice had been to the city of Atlanta before and was told to avoid the iconic shopping mall.

"Too ratchet!" Yolo grimaced and caught on. If this woman was going to be part of the family they were going to need to test her gangster. "Then again..."

"Glad I brought my Vaseline," grandma said to no one while Justice looked on in shock. Her shoulders shrugged since she was always down for the get down.

❄

"So what's up pop?" Sun asked once the kitchen and dining room were put back in order.

"This..." Killa said and turned his phone. Sun literally reeled back a few steps when he saw the disgusting image. His face hardened when he stepped back up for another look. He still wasn't sure what to make of the contradiction on the screen. Black men with nooses around their necks, yet smiling.

"Who did that to them?" he growled. Nothing is more offensive to black people than the image of a noose and its nasty legacy.

"They did. They did it to themselves," his father replied.

"You mean, like dude from Empire? The sissy," Sun wondered.

"Son, if Gucci makes a noose these niggas will put them around their own necks!" Killa snapped of the latest fashion.

"And these ain't even Gucci?" Sun remarked as he zoomed in for a closer look. The same closer look his father had earlier and came up with the same results of the designer behind what could become a trend. The racist win if that happens. "Raynard Starr, Atlanta Georgia. Let's go kill him!"

"We can't kill him for it," Killa sighed since it wasn't an eye for an eye. They were all very careful not to transgress because God hates transgression and oppression. "We can go kick his butt tho."

"Him too" Sun agreed and added the popular rapper who was endorsing the product. Asad had the kids out back in the pool so they set off to go kick some butt. "Kick it completely off his body!"

"Awe man!" Killa moaned when he reached the garage and saw the Bentley was gone.

"Bruh, how tough can we be rolling up in a minivan?" Sun laughed. Luckily he kept a car at the house as well. They hopped into his Audi and headed into the city.

Raynard Starr lived in the colorful midtown section of the city. High rent kept the crime low, or at least lower than some parts of the crime ridden city. Atlanta was once an urban oasis for young blacks but now it was just plain dangerous. Even for the most dangerous family on the planet.

"So, you like this girl huh?" Killa started with a rhetorical question mark in his tone.

"A lot! You remember when you first met mom?" Sun sighed, sounding love struck.

"Whose mom? Your mom?" Killa asked and laughed since

he and Yolo weren't exactly love at first sight. Especially since he shot her in the back of her head a couple times.

"Well, maybe not my mom," he said remembering the story Shyne relayed to him from their mother's diary.

"I feel you tho. When you know, you know," the wise father advised. "I wonder how she's making out with those chicks?"

"Trust me dad..." Sun chuckled as he recalled their meeting in New Orleans. "She can hold her own!"

❄

"Full house!" Yolo said when they reached the packed mall parking lot.

"I see why," Shyne said and pointed to a billboard of another popular rapper who was making an appearance at the local record shop. The gay rapper was on a gay crusade to spread a rainbow over the world.

"Oh that's just disgusting!" Diedra protested of the man made up to look like he was pregnant. The younger generations had become desensitized to such foolery the old folks were not.

Lil Nasty XYZ was a full blown sissy with a slew of number one hits. His antics got more flamboyant by the day. Now he was all made up to look like he was pregnant. It left such a bad taste in her mouth she rolled down the window to spit it out.

"Now grandma," Shyne began in the same tone she had heard a million or more times in her life. "Don't do nothing um..."

"Crazy?" Yolo offered and cracked up. They all cracked up at the notion of Shyne telling someone not to do anything crazy. Especially since they all were kinda crazy. She pulled up to the front of the mall and parked in one of the VIP spots, known as handicapped parking. Diedra passed her sign over and she hung it on the mirror.

"Pssssh," Shyne hissed at the notion of her grandmother being handicapped. Diedra was plenty spry even if she was in her eighties.

"Oh my!" Justice reeled when she saw four under aged girls traipse by hardly wearing any clothes. Their underdeveloped bodies were on full display and a smoke stream of profanities spewed from their mouths as they passed by.

"Do your mothers know you are outside like that!" Diedra fussed at the children. She figured they must have either snuck out like that or changed once they were already out of the house.

"Hold this," Shyne said when one of the children put a hand where a hip would grow one day. The first sarcastic remark to make it out her mouth was going to get slapped right back down her throat.

"Nuh-uh Mika," another one intervened before some sass slipped out. She lived in an abusive home and recognized the 'eat the cake Emma Mae' look in Shyne's eyes.

"My mama rat dere!" the child said with just enough sass to satisfy herself, yet not get beat up. The women turned to check the mama about how the daughter was dressed but she had on the same outfit.

"Hate it in your heart," Justice sighed to herself inwardly. She had been having trouble with her thinking out loud lately since she was around more people lately. She had grown accustomed to being alone but was enjoying the large family.

"What did you say?" Shyne asked with recognition twinkling in her eyes.

"My dad always told me that if I see an evil I have to change it with my hands. Change it with my speech," she relayed but Shyne joined her for the last part.

"At least hate it in your heart!" They both cheered. Asad had been reminding Shyne of that since they were children.

"This mall is ghetto but they actually have some really good pizza!" Yolo announced and got a strange look from her daughter.

"Really good as in trash!" Shyne grimaced and wretched at the thought of the cardboard slices covered in ketchup and sliced cheese.

"Well we are down south. Ain't no real pizza past Philadelphia!" Diedra added. Yolo smiled in satisfaction of steering the conversation away from Justice's father since she remembered how upset she got earlier just at his mention.

"We're going to the halal joint by my husband's mosque !" Shyne said and closed the deal. Justice nodded along since she was down for whatever. Also because a car pulled up on the little girls with the little clothes. A grown man smiled and flirted with the children. He passed them his number and pulled away before they got there.

"I'll take that!" Justice said and plucked the number from the child's hand. Shyne mean mugged them and they rushed inside to get a good spot before Lil Nasty XZY performed.

"Y'all go on 'head. I'm finna rest here for a spell," Diedra fawned and fanned. Shyne twisted her lips at the old lady's acting.

"Want me to sit with you?" Justice asked but Shyne was already pulling her by her arm.

"No, I'm fine. Mighty fine," she swooned like a southern belle.

"She's up to something," Shyne snickered.

"Why you say that?" Justice asked since she couldn't tell.

"Girl, that woman is from High Bridge! All that Scarlett O'Hara, I'm finna sit a spell!" she cracked up. Now Justice really wanted to stay but she was too close to where the rapper would be performing. She couldn't see but even hearing was too much for her.

"Y'all ready to twerk a lil something!" the rapper asked as he took the stage. The crowd, males and females all cheered and twerked. "Y'all gonna have to twerk for me cuz I'm pregnant! My dang baby daddy play too much!"

"Un-uh. I can't. Just can not," Diedra huffed and stood. She started in one direction until a devious decision turned her in the other direction.

"Sorry ma'am. This corridor is closed until Lil Nasty comes back through," a beefy security guard informed and blocked the way.

"Only because I'm black!" Diedra said loud enough to be heard by anyone close enough.

"Ma'am, I'm black too. It's just for a few minutes. He's only doing one song and he'll be gone," he replied.

"I be done peed on myself by then! Don't you have a grandmother?" she pouted and poked her lip out. The same way her namesake great-great granddaughter was doing to extort Asad out of pizza at home. It worked at home, and worked for her as well.

"I do ma'am. She raised me," he sighed. "Go on head. Just stay inside until he passes through."

"Thank you son," Diedra said instead of agreeing. She never liked to lie if she could avoid it.

Diedra waddled down the hallway like an old lady and dipped into the restroom. Meanwhile Lil Nasty XYZ tossed his panties off the stage. He had multiple stops to promote his new album 'My Baby Daddy' so he cut the free show after one song.

"Pull the car up!" he fussed at his manager as he dipped off stage before getting mobbed. The same security guard allowed him to enter the corridor, then used his massive frame to plug up the hall way. Lil Nasty switched his narrow butt down the hall while rubbing his prosthetic baby bump. "Shoot, I might be pregnant for real."

He was so busy fantasizing about being the first man to have a baby. He had enough money to get it done but didn't notice the restroom door open. He was about to second guess his decision to send his bodyguard to get the car from out front, until he saw the old lady appear. He was notoriously nasty to women since he liked men so much.

"You want an autograph grandma?" he asked sweetly, then went sour. "Nope!"

Diedra didn't find the dis very funny but laughed anyway before punching him in his nose. The straight jab busted his beak and made blood leak onto his blouse. He opened his mouth to protest but another jab quickly filled it up. She may have been in her eighties but that only meant she had been fighting for eighty years. One can develop quite a mean jab in eighty years.

"Help!" Lil Nasty XYZ squealed but the security guard was too stunned to move. He had seen a lot of things in his life but not this.

The shock of the old lady with the fast hands had him stuck. There was only one thing for Lil Nasty XYZ to do now, so he did it. Took off running out the back door. Diedra adjusted her dress, lifted her chin and walked back down the hall. The security guard gave a curtsy as she passed.

"What did you do, old lady?" Yolo asked knowingly when Diedra returned. She squinted and leaned in for a closer look.

"Who? Me! Why you ask that?" the old lady asked and shrank to appear even older.

"Yeah, she did something," Shyne laughed. They would have to see if whatever it was made the news. For now it was time to get up out of there.

"We should go..." Diedra offered and looked around. The band of trouble makers had made enough trouble to agree so they left.

"*R*aynard Starr lives here?" Sun asked as his father pulled up to a mixed use loft building. He had been scouting units in the building himself.

"Yup. Works and lives," Killa explained since he had done his homework. The designer was also a photographer and just so happened to be shooting an ad featuring the sellout rapper spokesman named Lil Doo-Doo. He was covered in misspelled tattoos since he couldn't spell too well.

"So we can kill two birds with one stone," the Sun nodded to his father then corrected. "Well, beat up."

"Indeed," Killa agreed and donned his afro wig and large shades. Sun did the same and they got out. The disguises were pretty primitive but worked to obscure their identity.

Both kept their heads down as they walked into the building to avoid the cameras. They walked up the stairs to avoid people and arrived at the loft. After listening through the door Killa determined it was just the two of them inside. He lifted his size twelve and knocked on the door Bronx style.

"Aaaaaahhh!" the gangster rapper screeched when the door exploded. He had been perched on a chair with one of the designed nooses around his neck. The start made him stumble and he was actually getting hung.

Sun looked to his father to see what they should do. It wasn't what they came for but they certainly didn't mind. Raynard screamed and tried to help but was too girly to manage. Killa shook his head and sighed. Black men have been fighting to keep nooses and knees off necks for centuries and these sellouts were trying to make it fashionable.

"Get him down," he ordered. Sun lifted Lil Doo-Doo enough to unhook the noose from around his scrawny neck.

"Thank you! Thank you!" the rapper said between coughs.

"Don't thank us just yet," Sun said and punched him in his face. "You're still getting beat up!"

"Did Lil Nasty send you?" Doo-Doo asked through the barrage of punches. "I'm not his baby daddy!"

"Stop!" Raynard shouted and tried to help. He would have been better off trying to help himself since Killa pounced. The 'paps' from the punches echoed around the wide open space of the loft.

"I, love, the, acoustics, in this, place!" Sun said in between 'paps'. Soon neither man looked like they looked when they arrived and their work was done here.

"Let me see another noose and I'm coming back. Next time I'm bringing my wife!" Killa warned as they turned to leave. Neither understood the threat but still got the point. They were going to leave those nasty nooses in the history books.

"S&S?" Sun asked since kicking butt always made him

hungry. Nothing slacks hunger like a stuffed burger and gourmet fries.

"Sure, but save some room for dinner," Killa agreed and off they went.

❄

"So?" Sun asked when he finally got Justice to himself that evening. The females from the Forrest family had kept her busy most of the day. They weren't exactly alone but he did manage to get her on the other side of the pool.

"So I love them! Oh my God we had so much fun!" she cheered. "I feel like I'm a part of this family!"

"Would you like to be?" Sun heard himself asked. It was sooner than even he expected and without any of the fanfare he was famous for.

"You mean, like, adopt me?" Justice asked curiously. She feigned a confused look even though she knew exactly what he meant.

"Nah, I mean..." he began and paused to kneel. All activity and conversation came to a screeching halt as Sun looked for something to use as a ring. A lone dandelion escaped the landscaper and was plucked from the ground.

"Aaawwe!" Yolo moaned and teared up watching her first born tie the stem into a ring.

"He gets it from me," Killa bragged. All of his sons were chips off his old Bronx block. Another win for Ogden Avenue.

"Plu-leeze! You shot me in the back of my head on our first date!" Yolo reminded.

"Uh, that wasn't a date. I was there to kill you," he

corrected and got shushed so they could hear the question and answer.

"Justice Jackson. I knew you were for me since I saw you throw that first punch in New Orleans. Would you do me the honor of becoming my..."

"Yes!" Justice shouted before he got to the question mark. "Un-huh! Yup! Sure will!"

Sun stood to get a kiss but the women swooped in and scooped her while his lips puckered. They whisked her into the house to cackle and coo like chicks do. Justice had a lot to learn and who better to learn from than three women who only knew one man in their lives. Plenty of women could teach how to get a man, only a few know how to keep one.

"You don't play!" Asad cheered and high-fived his brother. They had known each other their whole lives so he knew Sun didn't play about anything.

Killa nodded proudly at his son and all of his kids. He had taught them well and it showed. They were all go-getters and went after what they wanted.

❄

"*D*inner time!" little Diedra called to the men out back. Killa had done his part on the grill while the ladies did the rest inside. Dinner had now been designated as an engagement celebration for the happy couple.

"OK guys, I cooked the mac and cheese!" Justice warned. The woman who learned how to do everything else never focused on cooking food. She could make napalm from lighter fluid and washing powder though so it balanced out.

"And I helped," Grandma Diedra added proudly. This was another generation to pass the family recipe to. The Killa clan was old fashioned so the men were seated while the women fixed the plates. Only fitting since they didn't have to take out garbage or cut grass. The roles were clearly established around here.

Justice was all smiles and blushes as she delivered her husband to be his plate. It was piled high just like her soon to be mother in law showed her.

"Thank you!" Sun beamed back. He cracked a smile at her still wearing the ring he made her. "We're gonna have to upgrade this tomorrow!"

"OK," she shrugged. She could afford to buy a whole jewelry store if she wanted. The touching moment was muted when little Killa spoke up.

"Yooooo! Lil Nasty XYZ got jumped!" he said, reading his phone under the table since phones weren't allowed at the dinner table.

"I ain't jump him!" Diedra fussed and all eyes went to her. "I mean, whaaaat?"

"Un-huh grandma. Look!" the boy said and produced the phone.

"Oh my!" she chuckled as the lumped up rapper began to speak.

"Yeah, my baby daddy Lil Doo-Doo and his boys jumped me after my set at the mall. Him big mad cuz I'm keeping our baby!" he pouted and popped his swollen lips.

"Whoa!" Sun laughed since he knew Lil Doo-Doo couldn't beat up anyone over six years old. Meanwhile Justice looked at the bruises on the old lady's knuckles. She noticed them at the mall and this explained it. She and Diedra locked eyes and the old lady gave a wink.

"Well what is Lil Doo-Doo saying?" Sun instigated. He

kept it to himself that a little doo-doo came out of the closet when he beat him up.

"Right, here!" little Killa said since the next video was of Lil Doo-Doo. They both worked getting beat up to promote.

"Yeah, Lil mama XYZ 'ndem jumped me..." he whined, passing the blame back on the rapper. A sissy rap war was now brewing and their work was done.

"Enough of the phone at the table!" Yolo fussed and it disappeared back under the table.

"Have you told your parents the good news?" Killa asked across to Justice and got a stern look from his wife. The question was already out now so he just shrugged. All heads turned to Justice to hear the answer.

"I called my aunt. My parents are dead. They both were killed a long time ago," she explained in detail. The Forest family faces all hardened at the hard tales of the stray bullet that took her mother. As well as the crooked cops who stole her father.

"So, where is this Gwap and Tito?" Sun inquired harmlessly even though he had great harm on his mind.

"And the cops? Names please?" Yolo wanted to know since those were her absolute favorite bad people to kill. Nothing is as satisfying as killing killer cops.

"Dead," she said to Sun and turned to his mother. "They're dead too. I killed them all. One by one."

"Nuh-uh?" Yolo dared and twisted her lips skeptically.

"Yun-huh!" Sun and Shyne both agreed and nodded at each other. Shyne knew one when she saw one and Sun recalled watching her pick a fight with a whole crew in New Orleans. Plus she was packing. Only a Killa would do that.

"Knew I liked you!" Diedra laughed and rocked. "Now pass that mac and cheese!"

❄

"*Y*ou guys mind if I borrow my fiancè for a while?" Sun asked as he leaned into no mans land. The kitchen was neutral grounds most of time but off limits once the women folk entered.

"Yes, we mind!" Yolo said sharply and went back to their conversation. Justice was just getting to how Nuts saved her when she went to Tito's house. "So, a drone?"

"Yes ma'am," Justice said but Yolo twisted her lips to correct her. "I mean, mom. But I promised I would go ring shopping with Sun."

"Keep your word!" all the women chimed in unison. Honor was really big around these parts and if you said it, you did it. Say what you mean, and mean what you say.

"A man only has his word and his balls," little Diedra nodded up at her.

"OK, I'm gonna need you to stay away from your father!" Yolo fussed. Shyne slinked away since she knew the girl got it from her. Justice collected hugs around the room and followed Sun away. A goofy giggle floated in the air once he took her hand.

"I know a jeweler in Cobb County," he suggested after they pulled away. He left out the part about the man being the family fence anytime their work uncovered diamonds.

"As long as it's not that ghetto place they took me to yesterday!" she laughed. They went to pick a fight but only grandma got some action. The memory reminded her of the phone number she took off the little girls in the grown woman's clothes. "Oh yeah..."

"Sup?" Sun asked as she swapped the sim card in her

phone and sent a text. The text didn't get his attention but the determined look in her eyes did.

"Oh, this man, this grown man, gave his number to some little girls! Like your little sister's age!" she fussed.

"Grrrrr," Sun growled at the thought of some grown man trying to talk to his baby sister. The text came back so she quickly responded.

"We met at the mall..." Justice said as she typed. He promptly replied with a picture of his private parts. "Eeww!"

"Tell him you're twelve?" Sun said after she deleted the picture.

"I'm just twe, no, eleven," she typed. He quickly replied with a 'so' and another picture of the same appendage, from a different angle. This one was followed by one of his face as well.

"So, he's getting beat up!" Sun growled.

"At least!" Justice agreed and sent the one picture of his face to the database back home. She put her original sim card back in so this wouldn't ruin their outing. The conversation switched to happy things as they rode north of the city.

"Look, don't worry about the price," he advised when they pulled into the jewelry store parking lot. "You can have whatever you want!"

"Um," Justice hummed and looked at the dandelion stem on her finger. That was all she ever wanted plus she had a billion in the bank. She certainly could have whatever she wanted whenever she wanted it. She managed not to giggle when she took his hand this time. "You're all I want!"

"And you got me!" he assured her and punctuated with a soft kiss. She was still giggling and goofy when they entered the store.

"Hey! Mr. Forrest!" the elderly jeweler cheered when he

saw one of his favorite customers. Being a black man in the Jewish dominated industry made it an uphill battle. The Killa clan helped clear some of the bigotry in his path and he rose to the top.

"Hello there Mr. Lewis. This is Justice Jackson. My fiancè," Sun said with a timbre of pride that made Justice blush. The two shook hands and they got down to looking for a ring. In the end, Justice selected an understated diamond set. She still loved the simpler things in life and turned her nose up at the larger sets the jeweler and Sun were suggesting.

"Tell your parents to come see me sometime!" Mr. Lewis said after they concluded the purchase. Sun said he would and they headed back out to the car.

"Thank you!" Justice sang and looked at her engagement ring glisten in the sun. It may have been understated but the stones were flawless so it sparkled like Christmas lights.

"Anything for you," he reiterated as she switched sim card again to see what came back on the big man who liked little girls. Justice's brown face turned pale when she read the results. "What?"

"Oh, he's getting more than just beat up!" she hissed.

CHAPTER 7

"*D*avid Hudson. Age thirty two..." Justice read and paused to process the fact that the man was grown before the girls he sent pictures of his privates to were even born. He was actually older than their young mothers. "Originally from Gardena California. Served time for statuary rape. Accused of two more. Suspect in the disappearance of two..."

"Emasculator 2000!" Sun interjected and nodded with his suggestion.

"Do what, with what?" she asked. It certainly sounded appropriate enough even if she had no idea what it meant.

"I'll have to show you," he sighed since you can't really explain a thing like that. That meant taking her down into the armory where only family was allowed. His head nodded with his decision before it came out of his mouth. She was family. "I'll show you..."

"Sho nuff?" Killa announced when the alert alerted him to someone opening the door to the armory. He wasn't surprised to see Sun, but Justice was by his side.

"Yeah, well..." Yolo shrugged. "She is technically family now plus we can always kill her if things don't work out."

"Yeah," he agreed but knew it would work out. He saw the same look in his son's eye as he saw in his own.

"Nice!" Justice admired the hidden trap door to the stash. Not as fancy as her 'Bat pole' to her Bat Cave, but it'll do. Her head began to nod when she saw the array of weapons on the walls like art in a gallery. Sun nodded as she named them as she went. "Mac-11, Sig, H&K, and what the heck?"

"The original DC 2000!" he nodded proudly as she touched her mother's signature device.

"I thought that was a myth!" she admitted. It was only recently that she realized the Killa clan was more than folktales and urban legend. That realization made her look down at the diamonds embellishing her finger. "Wow!"

"I know right!" he gushed back since he felt the same. Then continued the tour. "Justice Jackson, soon to be Forrest. I proudly introduce, ``The Emasculator!"

"What in the Mortal Combat video game is this!" Justice reeled, wide eyed at the contraption.

"Allow me..." Sun offered and lifted it from her palm. He turned towards one of the crash test dummies and aimed at where it's crotch would be if it had one.

"Ouch!" Justice winced in sympathetic solidarity for whoever nuts got bit by it.

"But wait, there's more!" Sun proclaimed like an infomercial. Except it wasn't a second item free with separate shipping and handling. He hit the same switch and the chain attached to the mini bear trap retracted and snatched the stuffing from the dummy's midsection.

"Perfect!" she cheered and swapped the sim card again. David wasn't stuffed with stuffing like these crash dummies but was still dumb enough to give up his address. Along with another pic since he was so proud of it and all. This was it's farewell tour and he didn't even know it.

"Crazy huh!" Sun said proudly as they wrapped up the tour.

"It's OK," Justice said with a shrug. It was actually kind of primitive compared to the state of the art setup she had up in Brooklyn. It got the job and jobs done but wasn't messing with what Nuts had built.

"Just OK? This is the latest and greatest murder gear on the planet!" Sun insisted.

"Which planet?" Justice asked seeking clarity since he certainly couldn't mean this country. Sun just blinked for a moment before grabbing what they came to get. She gave a last look at the infamous DC 2000 and shook her head. "I need you to meet my family now."

"We'll fly up tomorrow," he replied quickly to stay true to his word. He said she could have whatever she wanted and meant it.

"So we can pay David a visit today!" she said with a sinister smirk.

"Davida you mean," he corrected since bruh was about to get emasculated.

※

"Oh, that's nice!" Grandma Diedra cooed when Justice showed the women folk her ring. Yolo squinted at it and marched off to confront her son.

"Small, but nice," Shyne agreed and looked at her own bridal set that looked like the Rocky Mountains.

"How old were you and Asad when you guys got

married?" Justice asked.

"Sixteen, but we got engaged in first grade," she said like it was the most natural thing in the world. In fact it was once upon a time. Before the world got complicated.

"What I do?" Sun fussed as his mother pulled him by his ear into the She Shed shared by the ladies of the home.

"Being cheap is what you did!" she fussed. "I thought you were going to see Mr. Lewis?"

"I did!" he insisted.

"I picked it out. I've never been into jewelry really," Justice explained.

"Oh, OK. I thought he was being cheap!" she relented and released his earlobe. "You're dismissed."

"Hole up, I never been in here before..." he said, looking around. Then down at the spread on the table. "Y'all got snacks and err thing!"

"Want me to set him on fire?" Shyne offered eagerly. She popped his hand when he reached for the fruit bowl on the table.

"Please don't!" Justice laughed. "Especially not before our first kill together!"

"Aweeee that's so sweet!" Yolo sang and teared up. She still gave Shyne the nod to set him on fire since he was now reaching for the shrimp. Luckily he saw it and got up out of there. The girls went back to their girl talk until it was time for Justice and Sun to record their first kill.

"Let's hurry!" Justice pleaded when they met in the drive-way. The phone buzzed again with more pics of his private parts every few seconds since changing the sim card.

"Gotcha," Sun said and opened her door. Justice cheesed at being treated like a lady by a complete gentleman.

"So, what do you guys do about disguises?" she asked as

they pulled away from the house. She waved to the family who stood on the porch to see them off as if they were heading to prom. Then again, a first kill is like prom around this house.

"Hoodies, wigs, glasses," he explained but she wasn't impressed.

"Yeah, we need to get to Brooklyn!" she chuckled and shook her head. They made chit chat to fill in the blanks of their lives from birth til now as they rode downtown to David's apartment. The love inched up another notch with every word. The mood turned somber and serious when they reached the hood. A sad reality is black neighborhoods are dangerous for black people. Black lives don't matter in most. Sun had brought along the Emasculator for their target but the twin forty caliber pistols were for whoever wanted some smoke. They made plenty of smoke.

"Guess we better put our hoodies on?" Justice suggested with a sarcastic snicker.

"Ha, ha. I can't wait to see what you got," he cracked dryly, then pulled his hoodie up.

"I'm here," Justice texted and he quickly hit back that the door was open.

"Bet this the last time he leave his door open," Sun said as they got out. He thought about that and added, "Last time he do anything cuz..."

"Hello?" Justice sang as Sun led the way inside the apartment behind his gun. Both had their guns high just in case but David was naked on the sofa.

"Oh my!" Justice blushed and turned her head.

"What the...You ain't no eleven!" he fussed and jumped to his feet.

"And that's your main concern right now?" Sun wondered

and looked at his gun to make sure it hadn't turned invisible.

"Can he put something on?" Justice fussed. She turned her head but kept her gun trained on his chest. One false move and she would turn him inside out.

"Yeah bruh, pull your draws on," Sun said since the Emasculator didn't care much about clothing. It was strong enough to even bite through Buddy Lee jeans.

"I'm saying tho..." David was saying as he complied. Both thought he would appeal for his life but both would be wrong. Instead he looked past them, looking for the little girl. "Where lil shawty at?"

"Grrrr," Justice growled and almost fired.

"Wait! Use this," he fiancé suggested and handed her the device.

"Just point and shoot?" she asked as she pointed and shot. Everyone watched the super sharp teeth shoot across the room and latch on to his private parts. David looked confused for a split second until the pain registered.

"Yeeeooow!" he howled but he really should have saved it for later .

"Now, press it again..." Sun directed as if the screaming man couldn't hear him. She did and the device snapped closed and retracted with his junk. "Whoa!"

"I know right!" Sun laughed at her reaction. Luckily his mother wasn't here because David would have had to eat his junk for lunch.

"Man..." he moaned and sank to the puddle of blood on the floor. He bled out quickly and reduced the earth's sexual predator total by one more.

"Now Mister, it's time to go to New York and meet my family!" Justice cheered. She booked the flights as they left the murder scene.

CHAPTER 8

"*C*oach huh?" Sun asked as they boarded. He didn't mean to sound bougie but it had been a lifetime since he flew in the greyhound section of the bus. "Yay!"

"Yeah I um, last second," she offered apologetically. She didn't want to come off as a spoiled rich girl to him. Especially since she hadn't revealed her financial class just yet. It was obvious the Forrest family did well for themselves but were regular, down home people.

"Yeah, it's not going to be a problem," Sun smiled but saw a problem right away when a man removed his mask and snuck a drink from a flask. The airline had cut out in-flight alcohol sales to cut out in-flight drunks.

"Please put your mask on sir," the stewardess asked sweetly.

"I have rights you know!" the angry white reminded as if anyone could ever forget. The angry white man movement was bigger than the civil rights and women's rights movements combined. Nothing is more dangerous than the angry white man. Not Isis, Al Qaeda, the Russians or Prussians.

"Right to get your butt kicked," Sun said to himself. He kept an eye on the trouble maker as the plane began to taxi. As soon as the wheels lifted off the same man pulled off the mask and flung it in the aisle.

"Whoo-hoo! America! White man!" he cheered and some more just like him cheered too.

"Oh boy," Justice moaned when she spotted another one. Before she could speak up another one had removed his mask.

"This must be headed to an angry white man convention?" Sun wondered when they were soon surrounded by mask less men. He made up his mind to mind his business and not to say anything.

"Please! Put your mask back on! FAA rules!" the woman pleaded and set off a round of rants.

"I'm an American! I have rights! I'm white!" they berated until she ducked and ran from the aisle .

"The pilot is going to turn this plane around," Justice pouted. She was so excited to introduce Sun to her aunt and Nuts but these nuts were going to delay them.

"Oh OK!" he sighed and stood. He promised she could have whatever she wanted and right now she wanted to get to New York. He shook his head and walked to the stewardess station where the scared woman cowered. A few more like minded men saw the look in his eye and followed him. "Do you have any duct tape?"

"Of course," the woman responded, since it was used more and more to restrain unruly passengers. Hopefully they weren't fixing anything on the planes with the stuff.

"Let's roll!" an angry white man, angry for the right reasons announced when the woman passed out the rolls. Everyone paused for a moment to commemorate when those words were said by a hero passenger on 9-11-2001. This threat was just as serious since they were disrupting the flight crew.

"What the..." Sun said when they returned to find the rest of the passengers standing to help.

The angry white men got even angrier when they were all duct taped to their seats. They mumbled about their rights from behind the tape that taped their mouths shut. Sun could make out the n-word coming from one taped mouth. The urge to tape his nose made him smile but he didn't act on it.

"Thank you baby," Justice cooed and laid her head on Sun's shoulder for the rest of the flight.

❄

"There she is!" Aunt Viola cheered when she saw her niece through the throngs of people milling through the airport. They were delayed by authorities coming to collect the unruly passengers.

"Mmhm," Nuts hummed and overlooked Justice. He wanted to see this man was who stole her heart. Nuts had known her since she was barely twenty and never saw this coming.

Neither did her aunt since Justice was never interested in boys. Especially after hearing the war stories that passed as love from Rashida and her other friends. There were plenty of love stories in Brooklyn, she just didn't know of many. The closest thing she ever seen like her parents was Nuts and Viola. Now her and Sun.

"Hey auntie!" Justice screeched and plowed through the crowd to hug her neck. Meanwhile Nuts locked eyes with Sun to see if he would blink.

"Hey honey!" Viola cheered back. She really cheered when Justice showed her the ring. "Oh my God! Look baby!"

"Mmhm," Nuts hummed about the ring but didn't look. He and Sun sized each other up while the women spoke. They intensified their staring contest inches from each other's face.

"Call it a tie!" Justice cut in so she could make the formal introduction. "You guys already met, but Sun, this is my aunt Viola. Auntie, my fiancè Sun."

"Nice to meet you ma'am," Sun said and cracked that megawatt Forrest family smile.

"Likewise!" Viola cooed as he kissed her hand like a gentleman does when he meets a lady.

"Mmhm," Nuts hummed more at his wife getting giddy over meeting the man who swept her niece off her feet. He was used to being the only man in their lives.

"Oh stop!" Justice laughed when the handshake became a battle for supremacy as well.

"Just making sure he ain't got no bi..." Nuts was trying to say but didn't make it.

"Nuts!" Viola fussed before he could curse.

"I was going to say bipartisan leanings," he laughed. There was a brief struggle to carry Justice's bag but Sun won that battle. "So, what hotel are you staying at?"

"Nuts! There's plenty of room at the brownstone!" Justice laughed. That was the first indication to Sun that they owned the whole building.

"He can stay there," Viola cosigned since she trusted her niece. She was grown enough to do whatever she liked by now. Her good upbringing narrowed those parameters to just the things that were best for her.

"So can we. Like she said, plenty of room," Nuts said and lifted his chin to indicate it wasn't up for debate.

❄

"*Yay!*" Justice cheered when Nuts pulled to her brownstone. No matter where you go or how much fun you have there is no place like home.

"Yeah, we're going to get some clothes. Be right back, minute and a half. Two tops," Nuts told Sun.

"Would you stop!" Viola laughed. They waited until Justice was inside before pulling away. "You really don't trust him?"

"I don't trust anyone!" he shot back. It wasn't totally accurate so he added. "I trust her though."

"Wow!" Sun gushed when they stepped inside. A single family brownstone is definitely something to wow about. He had been in plenty of brownstones before but most were broken up into a maze of apartments as soon as you walk in.

"Look," Justice stopped and sighed like she had bad news. She was too good to be true so Sun braced himself for whatever revelation was twisting her face up. "I kinda got a billion dollars."

"I don't know what that means?" he asked and tilted his head like it would help him understand.

"I bought some crypto currency with the money the city gave me for killing my dad. I was trying to get rid of it but it went crazy and I made a billion dollars," she sighed again.

"And, you're upset about it?" he asked, still trying to figure it out. He got the rest, that was the part he didn't understand.

"You're not upset?" she pouted hopefully.

"That you got a billion dollars? Billion with a b. Nah, I'm cool," he replied coolly. "Shoot, let's get another B!"

"Yay!" Justice cheered and hugged him tightly.

"OK now, your uncle will be back in twenty more seconds," Sun laughed and peeled her off of him.

"Nuts is, well nuts! He likes you tho," she nodded.

"How can you tell?" he wondered.

"Cuz you're doing that," she said and pointed to his chest going up and down with each breath.

"I like this dude!" Sun decided. "Show me around..."

"Um, OK," she agreed and set off up the steps. Sun tried not to look at her butt, but it was a butt and butts are hard not to look at. Plus, it was a really nice butt. No buts about that.

"This is my bedroom," she said once they reached the top floor. Sun nodded through the tour of the massive master bedroom. They made their way floor by floor until they ended back on the main floor. She wanted to show him the basement but Nuts and Viola came back. She knew Nuts wouldn't like it so it would have to wait.

"Mmhm!" Nuts said when they came back inside. "Let's ride Sun!"

"Let's," he agreed since he had a daughter and sisters himself.

"You better bring him back!" Justice called after them.

"Just going to shoot a few games of pool," Nuts said as he led Sun out to the truck. He asked a series of questions as they rode and Sun answered them all satisfactory.

"That better be the only thing you shoot!" she warned. "Don't come back without him!"

Nuts could tell from his diction, clothing and manners that he was raised right. Just being selected by a selective woman like Justice was enough for her aunt but Nuts needed to try him. That's why he was carrying on another conversation via text as they rode. Nothing tested a man like a woman and he knew just who to call.

"This hood came a long way!" Sun remarked when they reached the once notorious Fort Green section of the borough. "I used to visit my uncle Nelson back in the day and it was rough!"

"Yeah, they are taking back lots of cities. Pushing the bad people out to the burbs," Nuts replied. He once had a problem with gentrification but now saw the need. The powers that be should send the addicts and bad people to Mars and let the rest live in peace.

"I gotta warn you, I'm a good shot," Sun said as they entered the pool hall.

"Yeah, I'm a shooter too," Nuts said and got them a table. They both smirked at the meaning they meant and got down to business. "Drink?"

"I don't drink," Sun replied and got another nod. Drinking was legal but everything legal isn't always good. They made genial talk while trading victories by turn. A few games in a text caught Nuts full attention.

"I have to step out and take this. You can knock a few balls in and try to catch up while I'm gone." he said over his shoulder as he rushed off.

"Tuh!" Sun huffed. He would rather lose than cheat in anything he ever did. He took the reprieve to call Justice but got the voice-mail. He knew she was talking to her aunt so he clicked off without leaving a message.

"Hola papi!" a beautiful boriqa said as she approached. Sun looked around to see who she was talking to but no one else was near. She wore a tiny dress that could barely contain all of her caramel curves."Ju handsome!"

"Always have been," he shrugged and turned. He wasn't interested and the last thing he wanted was Nuts coming back with her all in his face. "Now if you don't mind..."

"I don't mind at all!" she purred and came closer. Sun blinked in her eyes like looking into the sun when she rubbed his chest. He looked over to the door, then grabbed her backside.

"Give me your number. I'll call you later!" he said and checked the door again.

"No phone. But you can come to my house!" she offered.

"Shoot, let's get out of here then!" Sun agreed. "Let me call my girl and tell her something..."

The voice-mail came on again but he had a message for Justice this time. The busty Puerto Rican twisted her lips to listen to the man lie to his woman. He had the double audacity to look her in the eyes as he did.

"Hey Just, I'm not coming back tonight. I'm going home with you dressed as a hot Spanish mami. I'll call you in the morning," he said and hung up. Meanwhile, Justice just blinked in disbelief.

"How, how did you know?" Justice asked in her own voice.

"I didn't, until I looked in your eyes," he admitted. The disguise was uncanny but he knew the eyes. "I fell in love looking into those eyes!"

"Awe man!" Justice cooed and got all goofy again. She nearly shed a tear and embraced him.

"Un-huh! I knew it!" Nuts declared when he came in and saw Sun hugging the decoy. This was his idea and he bet Sun would take the bait. "Told you!"

"And I told you!" Justice bragged on her man.

"Come on son!" Sun dared and twisted his lips.

"You did..." he conceded and pulled out a dollar to pay the wager.

"A dollar! Y'all bet a dollar on me?" Sun reeled.

"Naw Sun, I bet my life on you!" Justice said in her Brooklyn swag. She could do a lot of voices, languages and dialects but that one was authentic.

CHAPTER 9

"*I*'m going to show him," Justice insisted as her aunt walked in on her and Nuts fixing breakfast for her and Sun.

"I don't know," Nuts protested, shaking his head.

"But he showed me his, it's only fair I show him mine!" she whined.

"Showed you what?" Viola asked, scrunching her face like someone was being nasty. It had been a long, long time ago but she showed a boy hers when he showed her his.

"Not that!" Justice grimaced like boys were still yucky to her. They weren't, so a blush soon followed.

"She wants to show him our lab," Nuts explained. He knew there should be no secrets between spouses so he would prefer her to never marry rather show anyone their lair.

"He showed me theirs," she told her aunt for support.

"Well, if it doesn't work out..." Viola said. It was the unsaid that had them both surprised.

"It'll work out! He, no we, we're perfect for each other!" she declared as the 'he', in her 'we', walked in.

"We are!" Sun smiled. "Good morning! This place is incredible!"

"Thank you!" both Justice and Nuts replied proudly. Both had a hand in the plan so they had every reason to be proud.

"I'll give you the rest of the tour after breakfast," Justice said but looked to Nuts.

"What she said," Nuts nodded towards his wife. If things didn't work after seeing their secret he would have to euthanize the young man.

"Anyway..." Justice announced to separate the two conversations. She went to the chef-worthy stove and presented her guest's favorite food. "Just like your mom's!"

"Looks like!" Sun smiled at the omelette and hash browns on his plate. "The beef bacon is from the halal place on Ocean Ave. Their meat is fresher!"

"Thanks Just!" Sun cheered and dug in. Nuts and Viola shared a look at his using the family nickname for Justice. She was Justice with her friends but just Just in the house. He sighed and nodded at having to share her.

"I'll get these dishes," Viola offered once the plates were empty.

"I'll help," Nuts relented even though he wanted to go with Justice to make sure she didn't show him everything. Not that she could since there was always something new. He may have retired from the cause but still tinkered with his gadgets every chance he got.

"Come on," Justice beamed and took Sun back up to her room. Nuts just shook his head at what he knew was coming.

"I already saw this part of the house?" Sun remained when they reached her master bedroom.

"Uh, no you haven't," she laughed and activated the escape hatch. The fireplace slid to the side to reveal the pole. Sun had been in a few chicks houses that had a pole, but never like this. "You can take the steps if you scared..."

"I'm a Forrest , we don't get scared!" he called after her once she disappeared down the hole. He grabbed the pole and went down after her. Justice was waiting at the bottom grinning like a Cheshire cat when he landed.

"Who are you, Batgirl?" he laughed even though he wanted to go again.

"No, cuz what would that make you?" she fussed and shook her head.

"Not Robin!" Sun said and shook his own head. "My son had to call and ask what gay meant when Robin came out of the closet. They stole the innocence of so many children and forced parents into uncomfortable conversations little children shouldn't have to have."

"We can pay them a visit too if you want?" Justice offered sympathetically.

"Good idea," he agreed since someone needed their butt kicked. The moment passed the moment he looked around the state of the art lab. His knees buckled and he grabbed a table for support.

"I know right," Justice laughed. The funny part was he had yet to see anything yet. The Killa clan had been getting it in but their gear was primitive compared to hers. Theirs were literal sticks and stones compared to this.

"Wow!" Sun said for the next hour and they hadn't even reached the cars yet. "Yo, I wanna see how you did that mask!"

"3-D latex printer..." Justice explained and pulled up the

computer. The Spanish mami from last night was still on the screen.

"Can you do anyone?" he wondered.

"Anyone!" she confirmed. "We can make bodysuits too so it matches. Colored contacts as well."

Sun drifted into his head at all the mischief he could cause with this. First was pranking his sister. Her words caught up and he wondered why she didn't put contacts in last night. The loving look in her eyes answered the question but it wouldn't have mattered. He had no interest in the Spanish woman anyway. Real men are content with their woman.

"Not bad huh?" Nuts asked as he joined the tour. Viola stayed up stairs and out of this part of their lives.

"Not, not bad? This is bananas!" Sun reeled.

"I was about to take him for a drive," she cheesed and opened the door that revealed the McLaren.

"Breathe son," Nuts told Sun who swooned when he saw the super car. His knees buckled again but Nuts caught him.

"But wait... there's more!" she announced like an infomercial and switched colors. "Yellow, blue, green, fuchsia..."

"Red!" he decided and nearly swooned again when she went for the passenger door. "I can drive it?"

"Kinda," she laughed as he slid in beside her. She gave the verbal commands that started the car and opened the wall. Sun understood her answer when the car began to drive itself. He gave the address to their Long Island house and showed her where it all began.

All they needed now was someone in need of dead.

※

"*C*ome on seven!" Leroy Smith prayed as he shook the dice. He wasn't worried about shaking the throne of his Lord by praying on a roll of the dice and let them go. The big man had made it big on the football field so he didn't mind betting big when he came to Vegas.

"Seven!" the dice dealer announced when he struck again. A nod brought a pretty waitress rushing over with another drink.

"Thank you lil mama," he said as he accepted the drink with one hand and groped her with the other. He had been sued and slapped for this same behavior but it still worked for him every now and again. This was both a now and again because she giggled and blushed.

"You must be tryna spend some of them winnings?" she dared.

"Don't mind if I do..." he agreed and scooped his chips from the table. He had done this a time or two as well so he politely checked the winnings into the cashier vault for safe-keeping. He got special treatment since he was an NFL player, plus he would gladly give it all back to the casino when he finished. It kept his chips safe but that's not what the woman was after.

"You got a room?" the woman asked even though she knew he did. She also knew waitresses were forbidden from going to guest rooms. Good thing she wasn't actually a waitress.

"I shole..." Leroy was saying but stopped to yawn. He was going to need to hurry up if he was going to get his money's worth because another deep yawn followed. They made it to the elevator just fine but he was nearly out on his feet when the door opened to his penthouse suite.

"I got you big boy!" she assured him and dipped under his arm to help him inside. She was plenty strong for her size but most nurses are. She dug into his pocket and found a large roll of hundred dollar bills. The maid could steal those thousands so she tossed them aside and used a pair of scissors to cut his clothes while making a call. That was the last vision Leroy had before he went completely under.

❄

"What the..." Leroy wondered when he awoke in an ice bath. Typical after a game or workout but he had done neither. Plus a quick glance around proved he wasn't in the locker room, but still at the hotel. He leaned up to get up but several sharp pains told him to sit back. That's when he saw the writing in lipstick on the mirror.

'Do not get up. Use the phone next to you to call 9-11. Follow these instructions, or you will die' it said.

"What the..." he repeated and stood up anyway through the pain. He saw the array of stitches all over his body that explained the pain. Leroy was used to pain so he tried to lift one foot out of the tub. It caught on the side and tripped him onto his face. The fall restarted the internal bleeding that would take his life. It wouldn't have been much of a life anyway since he had been harvested of some vital organs. The body snatchers had struck again.

CHAPTER 10

Vegas police are reporting a bizarre incident at a hotel on the strip. A house cleaner found the six foot six inch, three hundred pound man sprawled out on the bathroom floor. Typical for black athletes and entertainers but this wasn't the typical drug overdose.

The coroner reports Leroy Smith was missing both kidneys, his liver, a lung, part of his intestinal track as well as his pancreas...'

"Again?" Justice grimaced at the grisly crime that was happening more and more. Body parts sold better than drugs and were far more expensive. Rich people paid a premium to skip donor lists so naturally a black market sprang up. The organ thieves had run through Central and South America but they were losing organs during the transport back to the States.

They especially targeted black athletes since they were usually in great condition. Plus some made themselves easy targets with bad choices. Now Leroy Smith's widow had to bury him minus most of his organs. The body snatchers were now officially killers. It was only right that some killers were on their trail.

"Oh my!" Viola reeled and covered her mouth. Nuts just looked at her, then Sun and knew what was coming.

"Oh my is right!" Justice growled and headed down to the lab. Sun hopped up and headed up to pack. They were headed to Vegas.

"Be careful!" Nuts called after them even though he wanted to come. Married life was great but he would have loved the chance to get his hands dirty.

"Ever wondered what it would be like to be white?" Justice asked when Sun joined her in the lab.

"No," he shrugged since being black was just fine by him.

"Come on Sun!" she challenged. "You ain't never want to have a white privilege fit? Ask for the manager?"

"No," he laughed since those things annoyed him. A slow mischievous smirk lifted the corner of his lip when he admitted to himself it could be fun. "I'm down for whatever."

"Good!" she cheered and held up his mask. "Meet Robert McCarty!"

"And you?" he wondered when she held up her own pretty blonde woman mask.

"Misty McCarty of course!" she laughed. "We're married now!"

"Those masks can come in handy after we get married..." he said suggestively.

"How so?" she asked and tilted her head. Sun laughed, thinking she was joking but the perplexed look said otherwise.

"So, Robert huh?" he asked to change the subject. "So how's the spray work?"

"Like this..." she demonstrated on her hand. Sun nodded

at the technique since he would be on his own. She retreated up to her room to undress and spray her skin. He stayed there and did the same.

"Jolly good evening guv'nor ," Sun said to the white man in the mirror. The blue contacts removed all traces of his identity and ethnicity. Now he needed a voice that matched.

"Um, we're going to Vegas, not London," Justice laughed at his accent. Sun's eyes went wide at her total transformation. With the contacts in he couldn't see a trace of the woman he loved.

"That's crazy!" he said and shook his blonde head. They collected a mini arsenal of weapons that raised his brow.

"Private jet," she explained, which explained how they were moving all these weapons across the country.

"Oh, OK," he nodded. They were halfway to the airport when she had a revelation.

"Ooooh!" Justice reeled and realistically blushed when his joke caught up with her. She shook her head and popped his hand. "You were being fresh!"

"Yeah," he sighed. She was a refreshing breath of fresh air compared to most of the women he met.

"OK," she said and held that same hand until they arrived at the hangar.

"Mr. and Mrs. McCarty?" the pilot asked to be sure.

"Yes. Paul, right ?" Sun said, sounding just like the pilot. Justice stifled a giggle but at least he found his white person voice.

"Thanks Paul," Justice sang as he collected their bags. The poor fellow had no idea how many times he had flown her to different locations in different disguises. They boarded the plane and buckled up for the ride.

"This is the only way to travel!" Sun remarked as the jet

sped down the runway and lifted off. He had flown private before but after that last flight in coach he vowed never again.

"I can act crazy and you can duct tape me to the seat if you like?" she laughed at that same flight memory.

"Speaking of crazy..." Sun said as he looked at his buzzing phone. He shook his head but smiled and took the call. "Yes, hello?"

"Sun?" Shyne asked and looked at her own phone to make sure she called the right number. She did so, now she needed to know, "Why you sound white?"

"Because I am!" he said and looked down at his hand.

"Whatever. Where are you?" Shyne asked when she heard the plane's noise.

"Who? Huh? I'll be back down in a few days..." he blurted and went to click off.

"Hey sis!" Justice called before he could hang up. She was looking forward to seeing her future sister in law in the near future. That's the thing about Shyne though, you have to be careful what you wish for.

❄

"Thank you," Sun said and tipped the bellhop who brought their bags up. They checked into the same hotel Leroy lost his parts at but didn't think the culprits would still be here. It was the last place they struck so it was a good place to start.

"Thank you," the man said of the healthy tip and went happily on his way.

"Welp, let's get to work," Justice announced after dropping her bag into her bedroom of the two bedroom suite.

She cracked open the laptop and saw Nuts had already gained access to the hotel security system.

"There's our guy!" Sun said over her shoulder when Leroy ditty bopped into view. They watched as he hit the cage to exchange cash for chips, then over to a crap table.

"And I bet that's her," she added when a busty white girl brushed her bust against his arm.

"Un-uh, her..." Sun said of the waitress who looked out of place. A nod from the dealer also looked suspicious.

Justice and Sun watched as Leroy rolled dice and drank the drinks the waitress supplied. They kept watch on the camera between him and the bar and saw when she laced his drink with the sedative. A few minutes later they headed over to the cage and into an elevator.

"That sure worked quick!" Sun noticed when Leroy staggered off with her help. There were no official cameras in the room so the show paused once they closed the door.

"Heads up," she said when the elevator door opened again and a mini surgical team stepped off. A white man led the way with a satchel. "Bet that's filled with surgical supplies."

"And I bet those are empty, for now," he said of the two ice coolers each of the two women carried. The coolers were actually filled with ice to help Leroy stay alive. They could only watch the door for a couple of hours until all four people exited the room. They had stripped poor Leroy like a car on Webster Avenue and left him in the tub filled with ice.

"He's a doctor!" they both surmised at the same time.

"I'll run a check on all transplant surgeons," she said and began.

"Between thirty five and forty five," he added and she added it into the search.

"This will be a while. Let's go explore?" she suggested. Sun had been to Vegas plenty of times but never as a white man.

"Let's!" he agreed and they set out for a night on the town. Neither gambled so they hit the club for a look. They had pictures of the people from the hotel in their minds and phones just in case. Those same faces were circulating through their database to see if they popped up on any other cameras. Most of the people were on the dance floor so they went down for a closer look.

"Wow! You even dance like a white person!" Sun remarked at Justice's movements.

"What do you mean?" she asked seriously and Sun knew she was serious. There are hundreds of things Justice does well, but dancing isn't any of them.

"Never mind," he said and looked for something to change the subject. He didn't have to look far. "What the..."

"Is that Shyne?" Justice cheered when she followed his eyes over to his sister and Asad dancing. She made a move to go over but Sun held her back.

"Misty?" he reminded and held up his own white hand.

"Oh yeah!" she laughed but not as hard as Sun laughed.

"Oh, we're going to have some fun with this!" Sun snickered. He kept an eye on Shyne and Asad until they returned to their table. "Follow my lead..."

"I'll follow you anywhere," Justice said to herself as she fell instep behind him. She couldn't see the smile from her words as they waded through the crowd.

"Asad! Shyne! Well hello guys! Here we are!" Sun announced when they arrived at the table. Asad and Shyne checked with each other first but both shrugged. "Robert and Misty!"

"OK?" Asad asked for clarity.

"From the swingers group. We agreed to hook up," Sun and nearly cracked up at their faces. "So take Misty and I'll take her. See you in the morning."

"I don't know who you are, or how you know us, but..." Shyne hissed the way a rattlesnake rattles. She didn't have fangs so she gripped the glass candle on the table. All that stood between them and an assault was a snicker from Justice. Shyne's head tilted at the familiar laugh which only made Justice laugh harder. She looked up at her brother and saw through the mask and contacts. "How, how did you?"

"She," Sun replied in his own voice. His sister stood and touched the realistic mask.

"It feels like real skin!" Shyne gushed.

"We could have some fun with those," Asad nodded and got a high five from his brother-in law.

"My uncle Nuts makes them. He can make anything," Justice explained. Sun was in search of an explanation as well.

"What are y'all doing here?" he asked.

"Same reason you're here!" she shot back. A million dollar reward for the culprits had the strip crawling with would be sleuths. It only paid out after a successful conviction so the Killa kids had no intention of claiming it. The body snatchers had left a trail of bodies all through Central America and Mexico. There would be no trial if they found them first. These were bad people who desperately needed dead.

"*W*elcome back!" Sun greeted himself in the mirror the next morning. The mask would definitely serve a purpose but it took some getting used to. It felt good to look in the mirror and be able to see himself.

"We got a hit!" Justice called from the living area of the suite. "No, a couple hits!"

"Word?" he asked and came out of his room.

"Yes. The waitress was spotted in a wedding chapel with the doctor guy. And one of the other women bought a car from this dealership," she said and showed him the video surveillance.

"Let's ride!" he said eagerly since he wanted to beat his sister to the kill. Shyne was in town so the clock was ticking.

"Uh, how about let's eat," she reminded since it was early and she was hungry.

"I'll call room service," he offered but her head began to shake while he spoke.

"Shyne invited us to breakfast downstairs," she replied. Sun twisted his lips but kept them closed. She said she would follow him anywhere so he didn't mind following her to breakfast.

"Hey! Where's Robert and Misty?" Shyne asked when they arrived as themselves.

"In the suitcase," Justice said and hugged her neck.

"Any leads?" Shyne asked and peered at her brother since she could tell when he was lying. She was so accurate with it, he just gave up on trying to deceive her.

"Yup," he agreed and picked up the menu to block her gaze.

"Girl we saw the waitress in a wedding chapel, and the other girl bought a car," Justice revealed and got a sigh from Sun. "What? We're on the same team!"

"Yeah, but no," Sun pouted but the cat was already out of the bag. An only child could never really understand sibling rivalries.

"We'll hit the car lot, while y'all check the chapel?" Shyne suggested. Sun shook his head but Justice spoke up. Asad shook his head too because he knew if his wife saw something she liked at the car lot he would have to buy it. Not that he minded since his life was dedicated to pleasing his Lord, then family. When done in that order a man can't go wrong.

"Sure! Then we cover twice as much ground," she said. Sun sighed again but knew she was right. The body snatchers were picking up their pace and needed to be stopped as quickly as possible.

"Anyway, you gotta see their lab! The mask are just a drop in a deep, deep bucket," Sun revealed.

"We're going to New York when we leave here," Shyne replied, then looked to her husband for approval. She ran her mouth but he ran the show.

"Great. I can show you the brownstone and the lab,"

Justice added. The two couples chatted over omelettes, then agreed to meet back there for lunch. Sun and Asad went to the parking lot to retrieve their rentals while Shyne and Justice waited in the lobby. Once the cars arrived they went their separate ways.

"Wed 'em and bed 'em," Justice grimaced as she read the name of the wedding chapel. She entered it into the GPS and the course appeared on the screen. "How romantic!"

"Probably has built in divorce court," Sun added as he steered in that direction. The small building was graffiti painted white to look like a wedding chapel except for the neon lights.

"Business is booming!" Justice said when they saw a few couples waiting to get hitched. One couple actually had on a wedding gown and tux. Another were dressed like Fred and Wilma. The rest were casual like Sun and Justice.

"Here to get married?" a receptionist asked and handed over a clipboard with a form. It was purely rhetorical since that was the only service they provided. Well, they served wings too but people usually got them after getting hitched.

"No, we just need a word with the chaplain there," Sun explained since it was the same man from the video surveillance.

"Only way to see Jack today is by getting married," the woman said and two more couples came in behind them to prove it.

"Fine!" Justice blurted and grabbed the clipboard. This was their only lead and they needed to follow it up.

"Should have worn Robert and Misty," Sun sighed when he saw their real names pop on the screen. The facial ID system pulled their identities from the DMV files. Technology all but killed fake IDs with real faces.

"Yeah," Justice agreed since it was the only way to see Jack. She filled out the paperwork with one of her other addresses. The ceremonies where pretty unceremonious so they moved along quickly.

"Next!" the minister said again and got them going.

"We need some information," Sun said with a hundred dollar bill and a picture of their targets.

"That's enough for the service. Info cost extra," he said and took the money. "Do you, Justice Jackson, take Sun Forrest to be your lawful husband?"

"Hold up, how much..." Sun interrupted but got interrupted himself.

"I do!" Justice blurted. Sun tilted his head like he didn't understand. She looked deeper into his eyes and explained, "Yes, I do."

"Do you, Sun Forrest..." the man read off the paper but now he got interrupted.

"Yes, I do!" Sun said deep into her eyes.

"With the power vested in me by the state of Nevada, I now pronounce you man and wife. Kiss your bride," he said to them and looked down the line. "Next!"

"Hold up!" Sun reminded, but paused to kiss his bride. She giggled and blushed through their first kiss ever before he came out his pocket with a few thousand dollars. The busy chapel made a hundred dollars every fifteen or twenty minutes. A few thousand was enough to make the man move.

"That's more like it!" the minister said and rushed into the office. He returned a moment later with a copy of their targets paperwork and handed it over. "Next!"

❄

"*T*here's Rob and Misty!" Asad laughed when he saw Sun and Justice arrive for lunch. They still weren't in disguise since they wanted to save it for the dirty work. Asad and Shyne had come up on some information on their target. They were eager to share but these two looked shook when they entered.

"What's wrong with you two?" Shyne asked between the two. "Don't worry if you struck out. We didn't!"

"Naw, we got what we came for," Sun said, sighed and added, "And then some."

"Yeah, Douglas and Sarah Bledsoe. He was a surgeon but lost his license over missing parts. She was a nurse in the same hospital. We got married. They live at 1290 Sycamore lane, Reno." Justice rattled off, but still looked confused.

"Good deal. We followed Miss Amanda Miller to her condo off the strip. She, wait..." Shyne paused to look at her own husband to make sure she wasn't tripping.

"Mmhm, I heard it too!" Asad assured. "She said they got married!"

"Are you serious! How y'all go for information and come back married?" she shrieked and pulled her phone. "Ooooh I'm telling!"

"I mean, we were going to get married anyway so," Justice was saying but Shyne had reached who she was calling.

"Guess what ma!" she shouted while Sun shook his head.

"Tattletale," he snarled across the table. Yolo stuck her tongue out and kept on snitching.

"I guess I need to call my aunt?" Justice asked rhetorically and pulled her own phone. She filled her aunt and Nuts in on the spur of the moment decision of a lifetime. Viola was used to her impetuousness but it always worked out for the best. She knew this would too since she loved her with Sun.

"Well," Asad said to break the awkward silence once the women were off their phones. "Shouldn't you guys be..."

"Asad!" Shyne laughed when Justice turned red. He was right though since they were newly weds and all.

"Oh yeah!" Justice growled and snatched her husband out of his chair. This was what she had been saving herself for so there was no need to wait another second.

"He's in trouble!" Shyne laughed as Justice dragged him away like a cavewoman. "Guess we may as well win this bet."

"May as well," Asad agreed. He knew what they did but didn't get his hands dirty but didn't mind driving. First stop was Reno since Justice and Sun would be busy for a while. Doug and Sarah lived in a gated estate with two brand new cars out front.

"Business is booming!" Shyne snickered to her own joke. Asad just shook his head. He knew she was crazy before he married her and married her anyway. All he could do now was enjoy the ride. She walked up to the gate for a closer look but only got a closer look at the guard dogs.

"Mmhm," Asad laughed when she jumped back. A second later both dogs were wagging their tails and licking her hand. "Dang, err body loves Shyne!"

"Let's ride!" Shyne urged when she hopped back into the passenger seat. Her urgency was explained a moment later when the killer couple came out of the front door.

"Looks like she's going to work?" Asad asked since Sarah was dressed as a waitress once again.

"We are too. Follow them!" Shyne said. They followed them to a casino to find their next organ donor.

✳

"**W**e can come down later and get a photo shoot playing blackjack," the manager suggested as they toured the casino they were performing in. The rapper was a little boy at heart and a toddler in mental capacity, so he had his work cut out for him.

"Finna win some money for my baby!" Lil Nasty XYZ moaned and ran his dainty hand over his prosthetic baby bump. He was really milking the whole pregnancy thing out until his album release.

"We really need to do a sound check," his manager urged, but got waved off once again. "Why don't I do it myself..."

"Poof!" the rapper laughed and picked up the cards he had been dealt.

"That's the one granny beat up at the mall," Shyne pointed out and laughed to her husband. Her eyes quickly shot back over to their target. She followed Doug and Sarah's eyes right back over to the effeminate rapper.

"Looks like they're watching him?" Asad offered while they watched them.

"I'm trying to figure out if that's bad or good?" Shyne asked. Her head tilted and genuinely pondered this new development. They were in the business of killing people who killed. As disgusting as Lil Nasty was, he hadn't killed anyone. "That doesn't mean we can't save him?"

"We don't," Asad replied when he caught her meaning. "Let's call Sun."

"I'll call Justice," Shyne said instead and pulled her phone.

"Hell-O!" Justice cheered when she took the call. She now knew what all the hype was about and was hyped up herself.

"I know, right!" Shyne laughed. "Where's Sun? Put me on speaker."

"He's here, but he's sleep!" she laughed but shook her new husband awake.

"I need to rest a little babe. I'm not a machine!" Sun whined and got laughed at.

"OK one, that's not what I woke you up for. And two, sis is on the line," Justice said and joined her in laws in laughing at her husband.

"Ha, ha. What you guys got?" Sun asked to change the subject from himself.

"Well, we followed Doug and Sarah over to the Casino Royal. Right now they're stalking Lil Nasty XYZ," Shyne relayed.

"And the other one just came in!" Asad added when the third party to their crimes walked in. Amanda didn't acknowledge her partners as she walked by.

"Lil Nasty huh? Let it happen!" Sun laughed. Dude needed dead so this would be a win/win for the team.

"We'll be there in fifteen minutes!" Justice said and jumped from the bed. She wiggled and jiggled her way into the bathroom for a shower.

"Better make that a half hour," Sun added from the wiggle jiggle of his new wife. He hung up and joined her in the shower. An hour later they joined Asad and Shyne at the casino.

"We're here!" Misty sang while Robert did a white guy chuckle.

"We gotta get some of those!" Shyne said determined.

"Asap!" Asad cheered and got his hand popped.

"Where is he?" Sun asked when he looked over to the blackjack table. There were players seated around tossing money but none of them were Lil Nasty.

"He went to perform," Shyne replied.

"Yeah, you said half an hour. What took you so long?" Asad asked innocently. Justice replied with a blush and giggle. "Ooooh!"

"Anyway..." Shyne laughed. "The manager is there, holding his spot."

"Sissies are like leprechauns!" Sun said of the piles of chips Lil Nasty had won already.

"There's Amanda," Justice said when she spotted the woman watching the manager.

"Doug and Sarah followed the rapper," Shyne added. It wasn't much longer until the rapper returned to the table and his winnings.

"Complimentary drinks sir!" Sarah sang as she swooped in with her tray. Both the rapper and manager plucked the free drinks from the tray.

"No compliments for you tho, ugly!" Lil Nasty laughed since he was a nasty little fellow. Sarah smiled at the insult, then smiled wider when he took a sip.

"Game on," Sun announced as Justice hacked into the hotel register. She found the VIP suite and printed a duplicate key card on the mini printer.

"Let's ride!" Justice announced and led the way up to the room. Asad and Shyne stayed put while the newlyweds went to do what they did best.

"Business is booming," Shyne snickered once more and slipped outside to do what she did as well.

"I think, we, we should, um..." the manager managed through a yawn. The warning was lost on Lil Nasty since his head plopped down on his blouse.

"I'm his doctor!" Doug announced and showed off his

SA'ID SALAAM

outdated credentials. Luckily no one leaned in for a closer look when he swooped in and scooped up the rapper. Sarah slid under the manager's arm and helped him away too. She laid him by the front door once they got into the suite.

"Let's strip this puppy!" Doug cheered as they prepped for surgery.

"Let's not," Justice said as she popped out of the back. Sun came out behind her and spoiled the party.

"Let's go!" Doug announced and made a break for the door. Sarah was right behind him but Amanda wasn't so lucky. A blast from the Taser seized her in the doorway.

"Aht, aht, aht..." Sun laughed and dragged her back inside. "Let them go. Shyne is waiting."

"What, what are you doing?" Amanda asked.

"You have a naked man on the table, about to 'strip' him of his organs and ask, what are we doing?" Justice asked incredibly.

"Drink this!" Sun demanded. He raised his gun along with the glass to give her a choice.

"Thank you," she said and accepted the sedative. Being asleep for a few hours sure beats being dead forever.

"What now?" Amanda wanted to know when the hand-cuffs came out.

"Now you explain to the police how you steal body parts!" she explained and clicked her wrist to the manager. Lil Nasty didn't weigh enough and she could have escaped. They left her nodding off in the room. A discreet call to the cops in a few hours would solve the case of the body snatchers. Meanwhile, Doug and Sarah were making their getaway.

"That was close!" Sarah sighed as they put some distance between themselves and the hotel.

"We're being followed!" Doug said as he watched the same

106

car make the same random turn he made. He made another just to be sure and the car behind them did too.

"Fall back," Shyne finally decided once she had spooked them enough. She watched them get smaller as they left town and entered the desert. Then hit the switch, "Business is booming!"

The switch sent the signal to the detonator attached to the bomb that sent the body snatchers into orbit.

he bizarre case of the body snatchers has been solved. An anonymous call led authorities to a Vegas hotel room. Amanda Miller was found handcuffed to a man prepped for surgery. The man was later identified as the rapper Lil Nasty XYZ...'

"Wow! That's crazy!" Justice reeled at the news report, but her aunt's lips were still twisted.

"No, what's crazy is you eloping!" she said and shook her head. Justice had always been impetuous so this didn't surprise her either. "You know we would have loved to see it!"

"We got the video from the..." Sun was offering but the woman twisted her lips to the other side to show him what she thought of the five minute video of the three minute wedding.

"Well, she's your responsibility now!" Nuts offered. It was done now, but he liked Sun.

"She's in good hands," he said and Justice blushed and giggled.

"So, what now?" Viola asked. Everything or nothing could change since Sun lived in New York and Georgia. She didn't mind sharing her niece but didn't want to lose her.

"Now, back to Africa. Our last trip got cut short," Justice said and looked over to Nuts. His mouth opened like he wanted to say something but all that came out was a sigh. "You guys could come with..."

"Yes! No!" Nuts and Viola both replied at once. "It's their honeymoon!" Viola protested.

"We can do our own exploring while they have their honeymoon!" he explained.

"Just sharing the flight with us," Sun offered in his defense and earned a cool point.

"Gambia is a beautiful country!" Justice offered too. Viola followed all the heads around the room and began to nod hers.

"It would be nice to get away from the city for a while..." she was saying but everyone jumped up and left her alone to go pack. "Guess I'll go pack.

❄

"*J*hope coach is OK?" Justice asked as they pulled to the airport. The looks on her family's faces cracked her up and ruined her joke.

"I forgot the duct tape anyway," Sun laughed as they bypassed the terminal and headed for a different hangar than they normally used. This one was bigger which explained the bigger aircraft.

"I um, invited a few more people along," Justice smiled mischievously.

"Oh no!" Sun laughed when Shyne popped her head out the cockpit window. "She's not flying the plane is she?"

"But wait, there's more!" Justice announced as another limo pulled in behind theirs.

"Oh no!" Sun reeled when he saw the smiling couple get out.

"Hush up and give your mama a hug!" Yolo fussed as Killa grabbed the bags.

"No thanks!" Killa said when the flight attendant attempted to help with the bags. They were filled with weapons and tricks of their trade along with clothes.

"He has his dinosaurs in there," Sun laughed.

"How about your mama and I can do more with our dinosaurs than y'all with all y'all high falootin contraptions?" Killa dared.

"OK, first of all, what happened to your accent pop? You sound more like you're from Edmund Pettus Bridge instead of High Bridge!" Sun challenged and the rest of the family nodded along.

"Been telling him..." Yolo said, shaking her head as she boarded.

"Y'all tripping! I mean, bugging. Yo," Killa called after his family. They were right though he had lost some of his Bronx swag, but he was still the most dangerous man on the planet. A point he intended to make with the pedophile ring operating in the Gambia.

The Killa clan settled on board the aircraft and prepared for take off. Nuts was busy on the computer looking for the right strings to pull and unravel the network of sickos. Each string made him angrier and angrier. Almost angry enough to come out of retirement for this mission.

"Can you please help me?" Yolo asked sweetly the second after the fasten seat-belts sign went off.

"Of course dear!" Killa obliged and hopped to his feet to escort his wife to the restroom.

"Awe! How sweet!" Justice purred at the gesture.

"Tuh!" Shyne laughed while everyone else shook their heads . It was refreshing to see just how naive Justice could be.

"What?" she insisted when she saw everyone's reaction. Shyne came over whispered in her ear and made her eyes go wide. "Oooooh!"

"My baby," Viola laughed. It was pretty funny but Nuts still helped her to the other restroom. Followed by Asad and Shyne.

❄

"Taxi! Taxi!" The drivers called out as the passengers filed through the airport. The Killa clan mingled in with the commercial flight so they would be solicited as well.

"We have girls," a tall Gambian man said and wiggled his eyebrows at Sun. Sun looked down at his own hand to make sure it was still attached to his wife's. It was, which made the solicitation even more egregious.

"Chill baby," Justice cooed and squeezed his hand before he reacted. It was a subtle reminder of why they were here.

"Got some young ones? Like, seven or eight?" Sun asked discreetly. The man's answer contorted his face before it reached his mouth.

"We don't do that!" he snarled as the nasty notion left a nasty taste in his mouth. He turned his head and snarled towards another fancy dressed man and spit that nasty taste on the ground. He may have been a pimp but drew the line at kids.

"Looks like he's our guy?" Justice said as she looked over at the man who made the first man spit.

"Yeah, go on ahead while I talk to him," Sun said and let her hand go. She caught up with the rest of the family while he pressed up on the pedophile.

He would have to wait his turn though since the man had a small line waiting to see him. A plane had just landed from the UK and he was busy booking grown men to small children. That made his death even more pressing. Sun looked around to see if he could get away with it on the spot but spotted too many people, cameras and security guards.

"Boy or girl?" the man asked when Sun finally reached him. He looked him up and down and answered his own question. "Girl."

"How young can you get? How many can you get?" Sun asked.

"From newborn to puberty and all in between," he bragged and smiled to show off a diamond encrusted gold tooth. Sun knew then that tooth was coming with him. "I have access to fifty kids!"

"We need them all! We're having a um, party?" Sun asked since he wasn't sure exactly what to call it.

"I just booked half," he explained.

"Cancel, I'll pay double!" he demanded, then decided, "Triple!"

"Where? When!" the man beamed and showed off that tooth again. His soul was for sale so the high bid just beat out the other customers.

"Tonight!" Sun replied and gave him the address to the

compound Justice had bought. They had too much killing to do for a hotel so purchased a whole resort. A private place on the beach for them to handle business.

"Well?" Justice asked when he caught up with the family outside.

"He's bringing fifty children. Tonight!" Sun announced and spoiled the mood in the family.

"Guess I'll take you to dinner," Nuts sighed since his wife wasn't about that life.

"I'll take myself to dinner. You stay and handle that business!" Viola insisted. A slow smile spread across her husband's face as he rubbed his hands together.

"You back in the game coach!" Justice cheered.

"Let the games begin then!" Nuts nodded.

❄

"*T*his is dope!" Yolo sang when they reached the resort. "Did you rent the whole thing?"

"No..." Justice sighed since she hated talking about her wealth.

"She bought it," Sun stepped in for his wife. They agreed to fill his family in so he stepped in to help. "She kinda made a billion dollars off crypto."

"Then, my stock portfolio keeps going up," she added as if the ten million more she had made somehow made her unhappy.

"Yeah, we did well off crypto too," Shyne said, looking towards her own husband. It wasn't anywhere near a billion but enough for their kid's kids and kids to live on. The Killa clan all nodded along since generational wealth ran in the family.

"Well this place will do more numbers!" Nuts said as they explored the resort. He was nodding but Justice's head was moving the other direction.

"I have other plans for this," she said without saying what they were. Everyone knew she would in her own time and focused on the issues at hand. The pedophile pimp would be there soon with fifty kids to abuse.

"Let's take them into the ballroom," Shyne suggested so they wouldn't have to see what was coming.

"Let them watch if you ask me..." Yolo grumbled. It would do those kids good to see what was going to happen to the man who rented them.

"Um, no!" Shyne fussed. She may have done far worse in her life but still recalled when her mother took them to watch an execution when they were children. She understood why, but wouldn't expose any other children to that. These kids had already been through enough.

"I'll take care of them," Viola added instead of going to dinner alone. She wasn't a killer like the rest but wanted to do her part.

"I can help," Asad offered and kissed his wife. Shyne beamed proudly at her husband as they walked away. Just in time as several vans began to arrive. They followed behind a spanking new Benz because business was good.

"Showtime people!" Sun directed like a funeral director. Even though Justice had already planned the funeral.

"Hey there!" the child dealer cheered when he got out of the lead van. His diamond tooth glistened in the brilliant moonlight.

"Hey yourself. Have them brought inside so I can pay you!" Sun said and shook his hand. The man rattled off instructions in Wolof and the drivers began to offload the children.

"We have something special for them as well," Justice smiled as the three drivers ushered the children in. She was fluent in Wolof as well and picked up every curse at the children.

"We have bottles for the young ones," the man said, causing Yolo to drop a tear. She was abused as a child herself so she was boiling inside.

"Not yet babe," Killa urged and held her back. They still needed information out of the man before he got dead. And he was about to get real dead.

"Where are the guests ? You gonna enjoy all these kids to yourself?" the man asked and smiled. He was a little too close to Yolo when he did and she lost it.

"Ugh!" Yolo grunted and socked the man with all she had, plus a little more from her childhood. The diamond tooth popped out and spun in the air while he went down.

"I got dibs!" Sun cheered and caught the spinning tooth from the air.

"Awe man!" Killa sighed since the plan went out the window with each stomp on the man's head. The drivers rushed back for a fight, shouting in Wolof and the fight was on.

"Welcome to the family!" Shyne said and handed over the signature device.

"May I?" Justice reeled as she accepted the infamous DC-2000. Sun twisted his lips since she was dissing the device at first. She never would again after firing at one of the drivers rushing to save their boss from Yolo's stomps and kicks. He wouldn't make it because she aimed and fired.

He was yelling something when the coil wrapped around

his neck and began to contract. His mouth was still moving as his head spun in the air. Shyne took aim with the new model and took off a head as well. Meanwhile, Sun handed his signature sword over to Nuts and hit the switch that lit it up.

"Use the force Nuts!" he laughed as Nuts took a few practice swipes with it. The last driver had no intention of sticking around and took off.

"Oh no you don't!" Killa corrected and clipped him with his foot. The driver slid head first towards Nuts on the shiny floor. Nuts took a swing at the top of his head and ran the super heated blade all the way through his body. He split the man from his rooter to his tooter.

"Wait mom!" Justice shouted when Yolo positioned the pimp's head between her feet. One twist of her hips would have snapped his neck.

"Awe, she called me mom!" Yolo gushed and blushed.

"We need the network!" Sun reminded and saved his neck, for now.

"Open this phone!" Nuts demanded with his laptop ready. Once he had access to the phone he would have access to the network of pedophiles. A minute later they had a list of nearly departed soon to be dearly departed.

"What we gonna do with them?" Yolo asked her husband since husbands are supposed to have all the answers. Even if it's not in their pocket they're supposed to go find it.

"I don't guess there aren't any pig farms around here?" Killa asked rhetorically since the Gambia is a predominantly Muslim country.

"Nope, better," Justice smiled mischievously. Nuts nodded along since she knew where she was going with this.

"Help me get them back in their vans," he said and

grabbed a man by the ankles. Sun grabbed another while Killa grabbed the other. He missed it the last time they were here but wasn't going to miss it this time.

"Can I go now?" the battered man asked below. It sounded similar to a Richard Pryor line and cracked the whole family up. Sun and his father doubled over in laughter while Nuts slapped his own knee. Justice laughed just as hard and had tears streaming down her pretty face. "No, I'm serious."

"Yeah, no. You're dead," Yolo assured him and raised her gun.

"Wait! I have a better idea," Justice interjected and paused his life once again. She turned to her husband and asked, "Can you load him in the back?"

"Sure," Sun quickly agreed since he vowed she could have whatever she wanted. The man wiggled and whined while he was being loaded in the back of the van. "Would you like to be knocked out, to make this easier?"

"Absolutely not!" he said as his final words. He was having a bad enough day already and didn't want to add a knockout.

"What's better than a pig farm?" Killa wondered as the men followed Justice and the women in the vans. Pigs were known to strip a body to the gristle in a matter of minutes.

"Guess we're about to find out," Sun sighed as they pulled up to the river bank. He would have guessed piranha, and he would have been wrong.

"Him first!" Justice announced as they all filed out of the vans.

"No! Wait! No!" The perfidious pimp protested since he knew what was in the river Gambia.

"Come here child. Let me show you a few tricks," Yolo said and summoned her daughter in law just like a mom does when giving a cooking lesson. She removed a large knife from her bag and explained, "It's just like chicken."

"That must have been the wing?" Sun laughed over the man's screams when Yolo took his arm off. She slung it into the river and set off a flurry of activity as the large crocodiles all went for the fresh meat.

"Let me try..." Justice said and took off the other wing. A large bull crocodile won the brief battle for that morsel.

"Here you go, fellows !" Sun said and kicked the screaming man into the river. He was promptly torn apart by the large reptiles.

"But wait, there's more!" Nuts said like a commercial. He and Sun grabbed one of the dead drivers and tossed him in. The crocodiles got a treat that night as they dined on the people.

"What about the kids?" Sun asked his wife.

"We'll figure it out?" she asked since she had yet to figure it out. Anyone who knows anything about Justice knows she would.

CHAPTER 13

❦

"Wow! Just, wow!" Killa remarked to the white man in the mirror.

"I know right!" Yolo agreed and flipped her blonde hair. She batted her blue eyes and could hardly believe them.

"We can have some fun with this..." Killa said seductively and gripped his wife's butt.

"Ewww!" Yolo grimaced and pulled away. "No!"

"It's still me tho?" he protested but her answer remained the same.

"Ewww!" she reiterated. "I wish we had these twenty years ago!"

"I know right?" Sun said as he came in behind them. His caramel colored skin was darkened to match the mask that made him look like a local. Justice came in behind him wearing the Gambian women's traditional garbs. Both had masks to completely change their faces.

"I wish you were coming with us!" Yolo pouted.

"I..." Sun began but his mother cut him off.

"Not you, her," Yolo corrected. There were so many

names on the list they had to split up to kill them all. Nuts would stay back with Viola and the kids. Killa and Yolo would shoot over to shoot up the UK while Justice, Sun and Shyne cleaned up the loose ends in the Gambia. A few of the European pedophiles had taken up residence here. They would soon become crocodile food as well.

"Next time," Justice replied even though she doubted there would be a next time. She had found her calling and was ready to dive in.

"Ready?" Nuts asked since he was the ride to the airport.

"To travel as white people, uh yeah!" Killa cheered. His wife just shook her head because he was having too much fun with this.

"Have fun!" Justice called as if this was a trip to Disney. The killer couple would definitely have fun delivering death to those who deserved it.

"We will," Yolo said over her shoulder as they followed Nuts out to the vehicle. Meanwhile the Killa kids set off to right wrongs throughout the country.

"You guys are in for quite an experience!" Nuts cheered as they rode.

"We've been to England before," Killa replied.

"Not as Dave and Donna!" he laughed. They all enjoined the beautiful Gambian sights as they rode back up the coast towards the airport. Both Killa and Yolo braced themselves for the abusive airport workers, but that wouldn't be necessary.

"Right this way!" an airport worker cheered with a curtsy. It was a far cry from the orders barked at them when they arrived. Both heads shook at the long line to be tested upon arrival and departure.

"Don't we need a covid test?" Killa asked and heard his

own voice. He cleared his voice and tried again in his white voice. "I mean, don't we have to be tested, again?"

"That's just for them," the man said as if his skin wasn't the same color as those them he referred to. It was their first taste of white privilege and they liked it. It got even better when they were passed off to the next agent. The white lady breezed them through the process that usually took hours.

"Thank you Abdullahi. I'll take them from here," the woman said and patted the man on his head like a puppy. The man was barely out of earshot before she apologized for his blackness. "I'm sorry for his blackness."

"Do, what?" Killa asked incredibly since he hadn't heard that before. That's saying a lot because he had seen and heard a lot.

"It's OK," Yolo chimed in. They followed her to a VIP lounge to wait while the common and black folk loaded the coach section. The food and drinks were free until it was time to board. A few hours later they landed in jolly old England. Once again they were ushered off before the common and black folk.

"Need our passports?" Killa asked the customs agent and prepared to pull out his documentation. He had to admit that Nuts was better than his guy. His guys couldn't turn his skin white and eyes blue.

"Tuh! You're white!" he laughed and ushered them through.

"Wow!" the killer couple exclaimed as a whole new world opened for them. The taxi to the hotel was free, as was the room. Dinner, drinks and every other amenity was comped as well.

"I can get used to this!" Killa admitted as he looked at his pale hand.

"Well, not me. Let's do what we came to do!" Yolo growled. She sent messages to every pedophile in the network and set the meeting for later that evening. She was ready to get back to her unapologetic blackness as soon as possible.

"We could have a little fun while we wait..." Killa suggested and wiggled his eyebrows in case she didn't get his drift. She got it just fine and scrunched her face.

"You could have fun. All I get is ewww!" Yolo laughed. "Besides, we need to go pick up our weapons!"

"Yeah," he agreed. Nuts may have had the gadgets and tricks but Killa was well connected. A few calls and favors had a small arsenal waiting on him.

"So, bombs? Machine guns? No, let's torch the place!" she suggested with glee. All those child molesters in one place would probably burn as hot as the hell fire. And that's a lot of heat .

"Nah, we're in England. We're going medieval!" Killa said with that killer grin. It was hidden behind the mask but his wife knew it was there. She looked at her watch and shook her head.

"Almost made me change my mind..." Yolo laughed over her shoulder as they left the room. The hotel offered free rental cars for white people so they drove over to meet one of Killa's connects. He had to send word ahead that Dave and Donna would be coming.

"Dave, Donna?" A dreadlocked man asked when he opened his door. He checked the picture on his phone and stepped aside. "On the table..."

"Baby!" Yolo gushed when she saw what was on the table. They were in the land of knights in shining armor so the swords were most fitting.

"These will do," Killa told the dred and picked up his sword. "One more thing. Chains and locks?"

"Ya mon!" the dred said and produced the rest of the items. They were all set and headed over to their appointment. The small bar was loaded with the network and their date with death.

"Where is bloody Lamin?" a man fussed and looked at his watch. The door opened but instead of the African man in came trouble. The Gambian pimp had set up the urgent meeting but had yet to show up.

"Lamin's not coming tonight," Yolo announced as she stepped inside. Killa was a step behind since he had gone around to chain and lock the back door. The only way out now would be in body bags.

"Well bloody why not!" a woman huffed indignantly. She was a stockholder in pimping the little African kids. It allowed her to put her own kids through college.

"He got eaten by a crocodile," Killa laughed but the looks on their faces made him laugh even harder.

"My god!" a man proclaimed and shook his head.

"Actually, he made out better than you people," Yolo said and pulled the mask off her face. The sudden blackness made the swords visible all of a sudden. It went from bad to worse when Killa peeled his mask off as well and was just as black.

"You can't be in here like that!" a man protested and marched towards them.

"Does he mean with the swords or black?" Yolo asked in utter confusion.

"One sec..." Killa said and swung his sword. The man's body took a few more steps as his head tumbled in the air. They both dropped with the thud that started the panic. Killa had to speak loud to be heard over the chaos. "I'm pretty sure he means black. Well, meant."

The crowd saw what lay ahead so they made a dash for the rear. They found it locked and turned back around. Killa and Yolo swung their blades in unison like a food processor and chopped them to bits. A red mist hovered in the air by the time the blades stopped spinning. They made a last check for survivors and stabbed them to make sure they didn't survive.

"For old times sake..." Yolo sang and skipped to the rear. Killa knew what she was up to so he extinguished all of the table top candles except one. It would ignite the gas from the line Yolo cut and level the place to the ground.

They stripped out the outer layer of clothes and headed back to the airport. Their work here was done and their kids had eliminated the network in Africa. If it reared its ugly head again, one of them would gladly cut it off.

"What now?" Yolo asked as the plane lifted off the ground.

"Nothing," her husband sighed with relief. "Absolutely, nothing."

"So, this is the end?" she asked to be sure. Killa just nodded because this was.....

The End

EPILOGUE

*J*ustice and Sun stayed put right there in the Gambia. The resort made the perfect orphanage for the abused children. A few of the children had parents but they found themselves on that list for renting them out. Sun didn't balk at the idea of staying in the beautiful country with his beautiful wife. They would split time between Africa and the states once they were up and running. They would add a few kids of their own into the mix.

Nuts and Viola went back to Brooklyn to continue their lives. Both knew he would be on call for the rest of that life. Whenever Justice called he would come running.

Shyne and Asad went home to raise their children but the work continued. 1-800-Killa was still solving problems the police couldn't solve.

Killa and Yolo went back to their quiet life in the Atlanta suburbs, save the occasional 'date night'. All in all the world was a safer place to be after a healthy dose of Justice.

THE SHAHADAH

A novel

by

Sa'id Salaam

CHAPTER 1

⚜

*T*he City is Atlanta Georgia, which at the moment was living up to its moniker HOT-LANTA. Not because of any musical act but the temperature above 100 for a third consecutive day.

Still, the block on the southwest side was a flurry of activity. Everyone is brightly dressed in the latest urban fashions. This was a drug block so the young dealers were racing to cars as soon as they approached.

Only in their early to mid-teens most could spot smokers from blocks away. Smaller children watched and waited until they were old enough to get a package of their own. In the mean while they begged what they could from the older boys.

Their female counters parts also wore brightly colored clothes, only in much less amounts. They too made several trips to and from the corner store that served as an unofficial headquarters for all things hood.

The corner store sat just off the corner that sold most drugs known to man kind. That meant the store too did brisk business selling collateral items such as lighters, beer, and cigars.

All eyes and ears tune into the heavy bass emanating from a souped up Chrysler as it bends the corner onto the street. No dealers would be running up to this particular car with palms full of drugs. No, if you were on this block selling you were selling for the young man riding shot-gun in one of his many cars.

The car glides on its huge chrome rims to a stop at the curb causing all speech to cease. All eyes zone in on the handsome passenger as he steps regally from the car. The young men take note of the casual yet expensive tennis shoes with plans to rush and get themselves a pair of their own.

The half naked young mothers all vied for his attention, but none got any. The wasted their best poses on a man who didn't see them. He commands attention by his presence alone. Its what's referred to as swag in the hood. Some envy him, some feared him, but all respect him.

"Hey Los! What's good shawty?" An eager young dealer exclaimed. He was excited about a chance to speak to the man who through so many buffers he actually worked for.

"Chillin youngin, what's popping out here" Carlos said genially as a politician, which in fact he was. He had the ability of making people in the world feel important because to him they were.

"Grinding boss! I knocked off a who..." The young hustler replied before Carlos walked off and headed into the store.

"Big Meeks" Carlos driver/body guard frowned and stepped forward. The young man already realized the mistake and lowered his head in shame.

"You know you messed up right?" Meeks boomed in his

noru abrasiveness. Even though he spent a considerable amount of time with his graceful boss, none rubbed on him.

"My bad shawty I got carried away" The kid admitted sheepishly.

"Do it again and you really gonna get carried away! You feel me?" Meeks said and asked. He wanted make sure the boy caught the death threat.

"Yes sir" he replied sharply showing some of the morals he was raised with.

Inside the store the busy elderly clerk brightens at the sight of Carlos. He had that effect on strangers but even more so for those who knew him. And Mr. Wright knew him better than most people on the planet.

"Hey boy! Where you been? Mr. Wright said cheerfully leaving the line of screaming kids holding up their unhealthy snacks.

"Sup dad. How's business?" Carlos asked matching the broad smile on the mans face.

"Not as good as it is outside!" he replied reaching to shake hands. "You looking more and more like your dad everyday."

Carlos clutches the mans hand in a firm shake as he smiles internally to match the external grin on his face. "So they tell me. How's my second mommas?"

"mean as ever!" Mr. Wright laughs. "Boy you know you in trouble too! You aint been by to see her in a month of Sundays!"

"I still don't quite know what that means, but I do need to fall through" Carlos replies. As he speaks he pulls a yellow envelope stuffed with cash from his waist and slides it across the counter.

Mr. Wright shoots a glance in all directions as he accepts the money. Mr Wright is and has been Carlos's bank for years. Conventional banks frown upon drug proceeds and require far too much paper work. That's why Carlos prefers to keep his money with one of the only people on the planet who had his complete trust. Mr. Wright had a more accurate count than Carlos did but never spent a dime.

Carlos didn't either. What people couldn't understand is his apparent aversion to money. His parents left him will off from legit business and insurance policies. That's what financed his lifestyle, he never used the drug money.

"Put that with the rest. What is it up to about twenty bucks now?" He joked. The total was closer to a million dollars than twenty.

"Yeah twenty two, twenty three somewhere around there" Mr. Wright laughs. Carlos produce's a crisp hundred dollar bill and hands it to the young clerk who manned the register when Mr. Wright turned his attention to him.

"That's for whatever they want" He answered causing the young benefactors to cheer loudly. The word spread outside in a instant and the kid's who didn't have money now rushed in as well.

The children mob Carlos with hugs and smiles as he wades his way towards the door. "Go see that old woman for she come looking for you!" Mr. Wright called to his back. "This weekend, promise" he replied as he steps from the store.

Outside Meeks is still scolding the young foot soldier about his error as well as anything else he could think of. When Carlos reached him he was chewing the kid out about a bad trade his favorite team made. Come to find out, that too was his fault.

The boy lowers his head again as Carlos approaches expecting to get chewed out some more. Instead a smile forms on Carlos's face. "What your name shawty?" Carlos asks towering over the nervous kid. "D.D.D, Duecy" He stammers.

"Is that three or four D's Carlos teases. The boy is so shook up he actually spells his name to himself before responding.

"J-J-Just one. Duecy!" he replied.

"You hungry shawty?.Relax lil dude why you so nervous" Carlos asked as if he didn't know. He was the king, he wore the crown and people were in awe of him.

"Cuz I, you earlier I ..."

"Don't stress that, don't do it again, learn from your mistakes or Meeks here will eat you" he said seriously. "Come take a ride."

Duecy eagerly falls in line behind the men and hops in the backseat to the envy of his co-workers left behind to sling rocks. "Swing by Lennox. Lil man gotta get his gear straight if he gone hang with us" Carlos ordered as Meeks turned the ignition.

"Sure thing boss" he replied with out a trace of the malice he had in his heart towards his much younger boss. Meeks felt some kind of way about not getting the crown once the throne was passed. He had put in work for a decade only to see this youngster get it through nepotism.

The trio arrived at Atlanta's high end Lennox mall and pulled up to the entrance. Duecy is in awe as a valet attendant come and takes the car away. "He won't steal it!" he asked incredulously. A new world was opening to him and it was amazing. "Nah they aint gonna steal it!" Meeks barks causing the kid to flinch.

Carlos frowned upon seeing it, He knew first hand that many ghetto children suffered from P.T.S.D. They witness so many acts of violence in their homes and schools and streets they were like war vets.

"Chill shawty, he don't know nothing about all this!" He snapped. He was growing as tired of the bodyguard as he was of him. Carlos has inherited him along with the crown. Meeks was a part of the royal court.

The men went store to store buying what ever caught their eyes. Duecy was amazed at the prices but Los didn't bat an eye. He spent money as if he hated to have it, and wanted to get rid of it as soon as possible.

They were a sight to see going store to store increasing their load as they did. Even in a mall frequented by singers, actors and rappers, the three street dudes made a scene. Again it was the swagger of the leader that attracted attention. Not all of it was good.

"Look at that buster!" Rip snarled as he and Rico watched the men go store to store. "I can't wait to bring it to him!"

"Be patient" Rico advised his underling, "In due time we gone see about him. The streets as well as that crown will be mine!"

The crown they spoke of was a gawdy platinum and diamond piece of jewelry in the shape of a crown. Carlos loathed wearing it, but it was part of the gig.

He got it from big Al when he was seat to a federal pen to serve from now on. He had gotten it directly from one of the original three kings who had them made, Carlo's father.

It was only metal and carbon to Carlos but men had died, and would die for it. The crown represented money, power and respect, for whoever wore it. Since men would die to poses it they would surely kill to. Men like Rico and Rip, even the envious guard to the crown had designs on it himself. Only the owner cared nothing about it.

"Let's hit up Sabir's" Carlos suggested as the car was returned to them.

Duecy notices it had been detailed while they had it and shook his head. He had been exposed to the street level extras that came with dealing. The weed, girls and tennis shoes, but having your car washed and waxed while you shopped was something else. This was the life he wanted for himself.

"Must have heard yo little girlfriend back huh?" Meeks teased. He had been close enough to the family to know details such as this. That's what made what was in his heart that much odious.

"Ruqiyyah is Back!?" Carlos exclaimed losing his normal cool. He heard it too and rushed to correct it. "I mean she is huh? that's cool."

"Looking like she straight out of Baghdad or something all covered from head to toe, can't see nothing on her." Meeks frowned. To him modesty was something frowned upon.

"She aint thinking bout me," Carlos said wishfully. It was more thought than statement but Meeks replied unknowingly.

"Her old man aint no joke! He used to run all the workers off the block. We just got tired of fooling with him and moved on. Them moozlums is all terrorist you know! They'll blow something up!" He insisted so adamantly you would have thought he knew what he was talking about.

"That's what I heard too!" Duecy co-signed from the back seat. Both men turned back towards him then back. The move tacitly said shut up so the kid did.

"Dude aint no terrorist, he's cool. Just protective of his

family. Them cats were selling dope in front of his people, he was supposed to check them!" Carlos said forcefully.

He flashed back to Mr. Sabir kind treatment towards him when he was young. It was him who took him fishing and fixed his bike instead of his own busy father. He thought back to the fond memories he shared with the entire Sabir clan growing up. The vision of Ruqiyyah's bright smile induced one of his own.

"Aight, you over there smiling" Meeks teased, "you gone mess around and get us all blowed up!"

CHAPTER 2

⤐

Life inside of Sabir's seafood was a flurry of activity. Having a reputation for the best fried whiting in the city meant business was always brisk. Ali Sabir was in the kitchen supervising and helping cook the days orders while his daughter Ruqiyyah and her best friend Hanifa tended to the customers. Both girls wore traditional Muslim garb consisting of over-garments, and kimars. Their attire was modest yet colorfully reflecting youth and style.

Ruqiyyah wore a dark blue over garment contrasted by pretty light blue kimar. Hanifa rocked a pink head scarf that matched her sneakers. "Shukran, as Salaam Alaykum" Ruqiyyah sang. Thanking and wishing peace on the customer she served.

"Wa Alaykum as Salaam wa afwan. Tell your mama I sent salaams and Insha Allah I'll see her at Jumu'ah." The customer replied as she collected her change and her order.

"Ok, Insha Allah!" Ruqiyyah called behind her.

"So what now miss college graduate?" Hanifa asked not meaning any of the sarcasms evident in her voice. She loathed her decision not to go to school herself and was immensely proud of her friend. "I know you aint trying to keep working here?"

"And why not?" she shot back curtly. "This our family business, our legacy. My dad 'bout to branch out and open more stores. Maybe even franchises! Shoot I'ma help him blow it up then find me a husband and make lots of babies."

"Well the husband part shouldn't be no problem!" Hanifa quipped. "Half the masjid done stopped by since you got home!"

She was tight too, being one of the most eligible single sisters in the community she created a boom in business with her return to the city. The vain brothers sought after her because she was pretty. Brothers with ulterior motives sought after her because she was a member of the well respected Sabir clan which also meant money. Even the more religious brothers vied for her attention knowing she was a very good reciter of Qur'an.

"Well you know a sister got it going on" she laughed and pretended to 'pop her collar'. That was another asset, the woman was totally un-pretentious. She viewed the favors from Allah as just that, which made her grateful and thankful.

"Girl you did not get no degree to be no housewife!" Hanifa exclaimed.

"I sure did! You make it sound like a bad thing." Ruqiyyah shot back. "Ummi got her degree in education just so she could home school us. Then went and got another degree online so she could help my father with his dream. Now look at them. She lives like a queen, spoiled rotten!"

"Not me girl! I'm trying to live a little, go some places, do some things. Won't no man have me barefeet and pregnant,"

Hanifa said practically spitting the bad tasting notion from her mouth. Ruqiyyah laughed to lighten the statement, but in truth she was afraid for her. Hanifa had one foot in Islam and the other in the streets. Being as pretty as she was Hanifa hated covering. She wanted to flaunt her looks as she saw other girls doing.

Hanifa, like Ruqiyyah was raised in a strict, sheltered Muslim home. Those streets she longed for would eat her alive if they ever got a hold of her. Ruqiyyah saw it happen time and time again. How many of her classmates had to drop out to care for unwanted, unplanned children. How many overdoses, date-rapes, how many good girls gone bad.

"I got this yall, hold tight" Carlos instructs as he unclicks his seat belt, and inspects his reflection in the mirror.

"You sure? I don't mind" Meeks teased, "I'll watch your back."

"Watch it from here" Carlos laughed," what do you want, a bucket of fish and a basket of fries?"

"You got jokes, Get me a twelve piece whiting, fifty shrimp, twenty wings and a diet coke" Meek said reading the menu from the car. There was a joke in there but Carlos, usually a comedian let it pass. He would never admit it aloud, maybe not even to himself but he was nervous.

"How 'bout you lil man, what you eating?" Duecy strained to read the menu from where he was seating. The delay made Carlos wonder if the kid could read. That thought disturbed him. In fact Duecy could read, quite well, he just needed glasses. He was just like a lot of inner-city kids who would have to get without proper medical care or nutritional diets.

"You get what I get, taking too log" Carlos said attempting to cut short the perceived embarrassment. Carlos checks himself once more drawing a snicker from his body-guard. He mentally takes a deep breath and gets out of his car.

Of course Meeks had a few more jokes and rolled down the window. "Say shawty grab me a bean pie and a bow tie.….. And one of them papers uh uh final call!" Meeks like a lot of people confused the nation of Islam with traditional Muslims. In truth the two were as different as night and day.

One had nothing to do with the other. Carlos just shook his head and walked into the store. He knew the difference.

A bell above the door chimed whenever it opened and instinctively the employees gave eye to it. When Ruqiyyah and Carlos saw each other time stopped. The delay caused others to take notice. Ruqiyyah shook it off and averted her gazed as he approached. He got into the line she was serving and pretended to study the menu. The same one he could probably recite by heart, having eaten there so much over the years.

"Oooh! What was that!? Who is that?" Hanifa whispered excitedly. She caught the tacit exchange and knew her friend well enough to see the sudden change in her demeanor.

"What was what!" Ruqiyyah demanded. "I have no idea what you mean.!"

"Whatever! You had a little moment there, I seen it!. He's a cutie too! Who is he?" "Change places, you take orders, I'll bag them" Ruqiyyah replied ignoring the question. Yeah he was a cutie but so?

The friends change places just as Carlos gets to the counter. Ruqiyyah stares at the ground as he stares at her. "Hi! What can I get for you?"

"Hey Ruqiyyah, can't speak?" Carlos asks ignoring the flirtatious smile.

✳

"*W*hat's up with Los and that girl? He must like her?" Duecy asks from the back seat.

"Los? Yall cool like that?" Meeks demands.

"N, n, n, I, I, I'm mean, I'm saying…"

"Aight, aight don't start all that again!" Meeks laughed. "Shawty he in love with that girl! Has been since they was like five. We all use to live on the same street back in the day. All them played together, He was real close with her brother but they had a little puppy love thing, kid stuff. Then when they turned like nine she stopped coming out to play.

Stopped going to regular school and everything, only time you saw her she was all covered up next to her momma. Anyway they moved cross town but Los always talked about her. Probably why he aint got no woman now!"

"Bet he gone get her now!" Duecy exclaimed. He thought Carlos was superman. But even superman couldn't over come Taqwa.

"She went away to college but she's home now. Her pops aint no joke. He be tripping about his daughters" Meeks advised.

✳

"*U*m…. Carlos right?" Ruqiyyah asked pretending not to remember his name. Their childhood friendship was as deeply implanted in her head as it was in his. That is part of the reason all the Sabir girls were sheltered at the first inkling of puberty. As soon as momma Sabir thought one of her daughters was even trying to develop she was pulled inside.

It was home schooling and no mixing with boys from that second on. If the world corrupted her children it would be despite her best efforts. Over her dead body if need be.

Proper up bringing told Ruqiyyah that the best way to fight temptation was to avoid it, with that she turned on her heels and went into the kitchen were her father was.

"Who was that?" The observant patriarch asked having seen his daughter flee.

"Carlos, he lived two doors from us on M.L.K." Ruqiyyah replied searching for something to do.

"Oh yeah! I remember him, good kid" Ali said fondly. He had been close to his own son he was like a second son. "Shame what happened to his parents"

"Oh yeah! I remember that" she said sadly at the morbid memory. "That was right before we moved" "That was why we moved!" Ali added emphatically.

❄

*B*ack at the counter Carlos is ignoring Hanifa's flirting. He was still watching the wake of Ruqiyyah's retreat as he ordered. "Let me get two number twos with peach drink and a 12 piece whiting, fifty wings and twenty shrimp" he said straining to remember the big mans big order. "Oh, and a diet soda, and let me get a couple of slices of cake!"

Carlos smiled brightly seeing one of momma Sabir's would famous red velvet cakes. Hanifa mistakenly assumed she was the source of the smile and smiled back at him.

"Is that all you would like?" She flirted earning a frown. Carlos was saved from responding by the vibration of his cell phone. He checked the caller I.d and stepped away from the counter to take the call.

"Sup shawty" He asked upon accepting the call.

"It's all good, real good" his worker Jay announced. "Just made rounds, good day!"

"Sho nuff? How good?" Carlos asked uninterested. He was probably the only drug dealer on plant earth who was not addicted to money. He did like to win though and since winning equaled money he was rich.

"Bout sixty looks like. I'll let you know for sure time you come" Jay replied. "Say you got lil Duecy with you?"

"Yeah took the cat out shopping, tryna give back" Carlos laughed. That was an attempt to downplay his intentions. Again the money meant nothing to him, he gave away far more than he kept. Even paid his workers more that another boss would. Normally high wages generated loyalty, but not always.

He paid out fifty cent on the dollar compared to the twenty or thirty cent other drug lords paid. Meeks and Jay of course didn't mind their large cuts but felt the street level dealers should be left hungry.

"What's shawtys story?" Carlos asked shooting a glance to the kid in the back seat of his car, no doubt being talked to death by Meeks.

"He's a good dude, a true hustle. Reminds me of a young you!" Jay laughed at the fond memory, then his tone changed. "His people get hit up too, same as you. Mom, dad even his lil sister. Shawty just missed it too, went to the store came back and everybody was gone" Jay said solemnly. So much so a stranger would never take him as the cold blooded killer he actually was.

"It was over on Cooper Street a few months back." "Oh

yeah! I remember that" Carlos winced as the details of the gruesome event came to mind. The family wasn't just killed they were tortured first. "What's was that about?"

"Drugs! What else" Jay exclaimed" some out of town dudes. Came to rob them and thought they were holding out. Shame how they did that girl, man they...."

"So who he stay with? Where he live?" Carlos jumped in to avoid the gory details. They were gory too, and for the young Duecy to see it would haunt him for the rest of his life.

"I heard he be renting rooms here and there. He aint got no family" Jay replied. "Shawty a trooper though! He be on his grind!"

"How old is lil man?" Carlos interjected.

"Fifteen, sixteen I guess" Jay offered nonchalantly. He didn't really know or care for that matter. He was old enough to sling the crews rocks and that's what mattered.

"Excuse me! Excuse me number seventy three!" Hanifa sings from behind the counter. Carlos checks his ticket and sees it's him being summoned.

"Aight shawty, get with Meeks later and swap out, I'll holla."

"Hold up real quick, I been hearing Rico and them talking reckless. It's time we handle them cats. Just give me the green light" Jay pleaded. He was a violent man and it irked him to no end that his boss was not.

Drug dealing is not for the faint of heart. When dealing in death one had to be ruthless. Carlos was not. He never gave as order to hurt anyone. He could not last in this game.

"Leave them haters alone. What they mad cuz they aint eating! I let them have all those blocks and they still griping?"

Carlos said firmly. He caught a lot of flack from his own people for giving up a few blocks with booming drug traffic.

He considered it a shrewd move to stop the back and forth fighting where neither side could make any money. Carlos was a business man, there would be no blood on his hands. The pause on the line meant Jay didn't agree.

"Aight shawty" Carlos said and ended the call. He return to a smiling Hanifa at the register but looked past her into the kitchen. Ruqiyyah sees him and steps out of view.

"Thirty one fifty please" Hanifa sang attempting at getting his attention.

Carlos keeps his gaze where he last saw her as he retrieve a large roll of cash from his pocket. He peels off a couple of twenty's and hands them forward. "Keep the change" he orders and collects his order. "Tell ya girl I said bye!"

"Oh you can't say bye to me" Hanifa flirts.

"Bye!" Carlos retorts stoically without looking back. Once out in the car Carlos hands the food to Duecy and takes his seat on the passenger side. "Jay hit, me need to bump into you" He tells Meeks as he puts the car in reverse.

"Yeah I just hollered at him" he replied, "where to boss"?

"Drop me off at home" He finally responded. "Then get to work."

"What about you shawty, where you want me to drop you?" Meeks ask Duecy through the rearview mirror. "He's coming with me" Carlos answered.

"Ok let's have it!" Hanifa demand as Ruqiyyah returns stifling a smirk. "Have what?" I have no idea what you are talking about. I had to help Abu" she replied. "Help your dad do what?

Girl you ran from that man! Now what's that all about?"

"We grew up together that's all, nothing more, sorry" Ruqiyyah quips getting back to work.

"Whatever! I saw how he looked at you. I saw you get nervous and hop the counter to run behind your daddy!" Hanifa demanded. Poor thing was addicted to drama and she wanted in on what just went down. "Plus he fine and got bank roll this big!. Left me a tip too."

"Keep that dirty money if you want, I know I don't wasn't to part of it. Do you know what he does for a living?" "Don't know, don't care" Hanifa shot back. "Girl you are too much!" Ruqiyyah laughed. "You know the sad part is he could be doing anything he wants. He was so smart when we were young. I use to teach him Surahs from the Qur'an and he would memorize them. He knew more than Hakim, they were best friends" Ruqiyyah said pausing to laugh at the reaction her brothers name had on her friend.

Hanifa was hopelessly in love with Hakim but he looked past her she was too aggressive for the reserve man. "So we use to say we was gonna get married and open stores like my dad" she continued. "He looked up to my dad more than his own."

"So why yall aint get married?" Hanifa pleaded.

"One because we was like nine or ten!" She laughed, "And two he's not Muslim! What? I can be a baby momma? "Well yall aint ten no more and he still likes you!" Hanifa said emphatically.

"Thing about men they all want what they can't have! Try playing hard to get sometime and you'll see"

"And what! Is that posed to mean?" Hanifa asked indignantly.

"Hakim! My brother likes you, you just scare him by throwing yourself at him" she replied sincerely.

"I'ma asks him to marry me soon as he come!"

"See! That's what I mean" Ruqiyyah shook her head. "In a perfect world Carlos would be named Malik. He would be hafiz of Qur'an, own and operate legitimate business."

"Well Allah is the best of planners, make Du'aa maybe that can happen" Hanifa said seriously. Ruqiyyah didn't reply. She was busy making Du'aa.

CHAPTER 3

eeks pulls into the drive way of Carlos modest home and parks. They all exit and Meeks gets into his custom S.U.V as Carlos leads Duecy towards the house.

Duecy stares wide eyed around the living room as the take seats in front of a large flat screen T.V. Carlos began pulling the food from the bag and serves his guest. He pulls the crown medallion off his neck and tossing it on the coffee table. "Got ya eyes on the prize I see" Carlos announced seeing Duecy fixated on the chain.

"That fiyah! You wear the crown!" He announced in awe. He couldn't believe how his day was going. Only that morning he awoke alone in a boarding house full of strangers. At fifteen there would be on school, no breakfast, no love. He got dressed and hit the block to earn his daily bread. Now he sat in the presence of who he wanted to be. The King!

"Man, you can have it and all the stress that comes along with it." Carlos sighed.

"I would love that!" Duecy exclaimed. "I would hold it down too!"

"You think so huh? Thing about being on top is you got everyone shooting at you. Sometimes literally. You can't trust no one, absolutely no one! Sound like fun?"

"You can trust me!" Duecy swore. "Is it true you cut a mans head off!"

"Is that what they are saying now?" Carlos laughed heartily. "Be careful about repeating everything you hear. It will make you a liar more often than not!. I guess that's better that the real story though."

"So how did you get it?" Duecy asked in between gulps of food. Carlos saw how he devoured the food and knew it was most likely his first meal of the day.

"You want the real story or the legend?" Carlos asked finally taking a bit of his own food.

"guess I already know the rumors, let's hear what really went down."

"You heard of Big Al right?" Carlos began. "mm hmp!" Duecy nodded with a mouthful of food. "Well, before he went to prison he gave it to me" "And!" Duecy exclaimed having to force his food down to ask. "That's it! Just gave it to you? No drama? Nobody head got cut off!"

"No beheadings but plenty of Drama. Big Al took it from a guy named Mo-Jo when he passed" Carlos said with the gravity of the grim situation engraved in his contorted face. "What did Mo-Jo pass from?" Duecy asked eagerly

"from Big Al!" Carlos shot back.

"Where did Mo-Jo get the chain from? "

"From my dad. He had them made. Him and his two closet friends use to run this city. Not just a few blocks or neighborhoods like us, but the entire city of Atlanta! Jim, Mr.

Wright down at the store and another dude they called breeze."

"Wait! Mr. Wright from the store? The mean old man?" Duecy asks incredulously. "I can't see it!"

"Believe it! The three kings! They had the crowns made cuz they were the kings! Then one day Mr. Wright got bagged and breeze disappeared. My dad stayed down until... Well he got killed! Him and my mom"

"I feel you, my mom, dad and little sister all got killed. She was only nine" Duecy replied. He didn't bother trying to wipe away the lone tear that escaped.

They both sat in silence for a few minutes caught up in their own painful memories finally Carlos shook it off and went on. "So whoever did it, you know, my parents they took the chain and medallion when they did. No one knew who did it until a few years back when Mo-Jo started wearing it. When Big Al heard he caught up with him in the park and took it from him. Along with his life" Carlos looked shaken as he recounted the event.

"So how you get it?" Duecy asked totally enthralled.

"I was right there. He made me come then handed it to me. It still had blood on it. He yelled at me to put it on and never take it off. I did. I was the king from that moment on, weather I wanted to or not" Carlos said.

"That's why Big Al went to jail? He couldn't get away?" Duecy demanded.

"He didn't try, just waited for the police. He wanted to make a point, he did too cuz everyone deferred to me, as king.

Duecy was confused by his saddened demeanor, who wouldn't want to be king?

"Mo-Jo's nephew Rico was out there too. I could tell he

didn't like what happened but wasn't really much he could do about it. Not only did I inherit the business but the security as well. That's why Big Meeks is always around" Carlos continued.

"Shoot let him try something! And I'll..."

"You'll what? Throw away your life too?" Carlos cut in, "spend the rest of your days being told what to do. Have the blood of a human being on your hands?"

"No, I didn't think about all that" Duecy said wistfully. Those were same words that were being said around the country in its state pens, Too late once the judge bangs that gravel.

❄

*M*eeks pulls into the crowded park and scans the area. He spots Jays truck near the courts were a game is in session, He swings his on S.U.V over where Jay is and parks next to him. "You doing it like that!" Big Meeks asks upon seeing Jay's truck is outfitted with new twenty four inch rims. The cost of the rims and tires alone would pay for a nice car.

"Yeah biz is good!" Jay shoots back and the men laugh heartily at the lucrative inside joke. During the revelry Meeks gets out of his own truck and into Jay's.

"What we looking like?" Meeks asked eagerly.

"Right at sixty, good day" Jay replies.

"I'm sorry, I couldn't hear you. Fifty did you say"

"Well that's after! But we still can?" Jay offers.

"Fifty it is" Meeks decides, instructing him to skim another ten thousand off the already short money.

"Robin hood wont miss it, probably gonna give it all away

anyway" Jay adds. It was his way of justifying stealing from the Tally.

After splitting up what they skimmed off the top Meeks put fifty thousand drug dollars into a bag to give to Carlos. He pocketed seven thousand for himself. While Jay kept ten, there was no honor among thieves.

❄

*J*ay and Meeks weren't the only ones plotting on Carlos. Across town he was being discussed in even less friendly conversation. Rip was nodding his head to the latest song depicting drugs and violence. The rapper made illicit life seem fun. Rico wasn't listening; he was consumed with his own envious thoughts.

"What's up player? You look like a caged lion, all that pacing" Rip said cutting the sound.

"I'm saying though, them cats ass buying out the mall while we struggling!" Rico lamented. "We far from struggling" RIP laughed" but them cats is eating good."

"Eating off my plate! My food!" Rico shot back hotly.

"So let's move on them. Dude soft! Carlos aint put in no work! He's soft, you letting them breath!"

"Oh so you run things now? You the boss" Rico fumed. "Dude wearing the crown off my uncle neck. I'm supposed to have it, I should be king! This aint just business, it's personal!"

'Personal for you' Rip thinks to himself. He was tired of the personal beef that was costing him money, for him it always business, never personal. That's why he set wheels in motion on his own.

"You da man" Rip says bordering on sarcasm. "I'm 'bout to hit these streets and see what's shaking out there feel me?"

"I feel you" Rico says calming back down. He gives his partner in crime a hug as he stands to leave. "Let's hook up later, hit a club."

"That's what's up" Rip agrees. Once in his car he dials 'plan B' on his cell phone.

"What's good?" Meeks replies upon answering.

"You tell me, I'm ready. Past Ready!"

"Be patient" Meeks says as he pulls in to Carlos driveway "I'll let you know just be ready on your end" Meeks disconnects the call with out waiting for a reply. He grabs the bag of money and exits his vehicle.

"Get that" Carlos ordered softly when the doorbell rings. He intends to get Duecy acclimated to what was soon to be his new position within the organization. Duecy eager to please leaps from his seat and rushes to open the door.

"You don't ask who it is before you open doors!" Meeks boomed down at the kid. "What if I was a jacker, or police?"

"I, I, I... "

"Shut up and get out the way!" He demanded barging in.

"Be easy, he's just a kid" Carlos instructs.

"Then he needs to stay in his place!" Meeks shoots back, "Matter fact find something to do grown folks is about to talk!"

"He cool, have a seat Duecy" Carlos orders. In fact he was about to dismiss him himself until 'the help' came in barking orders. The sight of the coveted crown laying on the coffee table momentarily distracts Meeks as he is seated. He wanted it as bad as Rico, and was setting as plan in motion to secure it for himself.

He passes the money bag to his boss and watches him.

Carlos shakes his head as he finishes the first count. It's not until a second count confirms the first that he speaks up.

"This is short, way short!" He says hotly. His not caring about the money was not a green light to steal it. "I pay way too much for people…. To be stealing from me!"

"How much?" Meeks ask with mock surprise.

"Over twenty according to what the spots reported turning in! Jay is back in a spot, you make the pick ups from now on!"

"Me! So I'm getting demoted too?" Meeks ask sounding wounded.

"That's money out of your pocket too! You should be more concerned. It bothers me you're your not" Carlos replied. An awkward silence follows the tacit accusation. Los put it out there so Meeks could deny it, or defend himself. He didn't.

"I'll do it if you want" Duecy offered helpfully. "Shut up! I already told you this grown folks B.I. stay in your lane!" Meeks barked.

"Be easy, he's just trying to help. Help a situation that shouldn't even be" Carlos said plainly. "I can trust you to make sure the money is straight, can't I?"

"Um yeah sure" Meeks said unconvincingly.

"That's what's up. We're losing too much money. Get it straight."

"Cool boss" Meeks replied taking to his feet. He shoots Duecy a cold glance, and then walks to the door. "Be easy."

"You too" Carlos replies with out feeling. The cat was out of the bag now so even forced cordiality wasn't an option.

"I mean it Los, I'll do whatever you need me to do, just say the word." Duecy says as soon as the door closed behind Meeks.

"Actually I'm glad to hear you say that" Carlos announced cheerfully." You're your cut off! No more hustling for you."

"Because of the slip up earlier?" Duecy asked solemnly, referring to speaking business out in public.

"Well that's part of it. You can't slip up in this game. There's no room for error, slip ups will get you in jail or a grave and I don't think either one of these places are fun" he replied plainly.

"I aint got nothing else" the kid whined, now sounding his age. "I hustle to eat! I aint got no family, no where to stay, nothing!

"Sure you do! I'm your family, and you're staying here!" Carlos said having just decided. "You're going back to school. We'll go get your stuff after I whip you in this game."

"Beat me?" Duecy laughs grabbing the game controllers, "in your dreams.

CHAPTER 4

⠀⠀⠀⠀⠀⠀⠀⠀⠀⠀⠀⠀⠀⠀⠀⠀⠀⠀⠀⠀⠀⠀

*R*ip was typing furiously on his smart phones keyboard trying to manage four text conversations at once. Who ever said dealing drugs was easy could never understood the mechanics of it. Going against the natural disposition God gave you to distinguish wrong from right is stressful in itself.

It's a twenty four hour job dealing with people who can not and should not be trusted. There is no 401k or health plan. The only retirement plan is prison, or dead. There is no honor among thieves, but how could there be. Its an oxymoron.

Of course there are great riches to be had, but it's not worth it. The ends don't justify the means. It's like what Allah says in the Qur'an: "In them is a great sin and some benefits for men, but the sin is greater that the benefits."

Meeks walks into the dimly lit bar and spots him illuminated by the phones bright screen. He makes his way over to the booth and slides in. Sup?" Rip asked looking up from his phone for a split second. "Chillin, what you got going?" He asked, curious about the mans dilemma.

"Baby mama drama, times four" he sighed. "Anyway, what's good? I'm ready on my end" Rip announces turning the phone off. His children and their needs would have to wait.

"Almost ready too, we have a little situation so we may have to move quicker than expected" Meeks replies. Of course the situation was his being suspected of stealing. He planned to skim as much as he could get away with before he took over. It was a matter of principal, and he had none.

"Well what's the hold up?" Rip complains, bitterly. "I sick of playing side kick to this guy! All he's concerned with is that silly crown. If I get a hold of it I would melt it down and sell it. This is business, not personal!"

"I feel your pain. I'm sick of being the hype man for Robin hood" Meeks laments, "This guys cares nothing about the money. I watched him give away every penny he took in once, didn't keep nare coin for himself. He got that trust fund and acts as if he's too good for this dirty money."

"The dirtier the better as far as I'm concerned" Rip laughs, "I aint got no morals. When my mamma started using I sold to her too!"

Meeks was as morally bankrupt as he was and laughed along with him. Half of his immediate family used drugs so he was immune to the misery.

"So how you wanna do this?" Meeks asks.

"Rico got a big shipment coming in. He's waiting on that before he makes his move on your man. Gotta make sure he got the work to handle the newly inherited territory" Rip explains. "While he does that, you guys take care of Rico."

"Sounds like a plan. You guys need to send a team to hit

Carlos's bank as well. No sense in letting the old man keep all that dough" Meeks conspires, "well split that and both wear the crown."

"How we both gonna were it? Take turns? Rip ask. "There's only on crown."

"Nah, actually there are two. The other in the bank with the money" Meeks drools.

❄

"What do you see?" Carlos asks Duecy as they ride through the ghetto. The transition from Carlos's neighborhood is a sudden drastic change. He lives in a small subdivision full of proud homeowners, lawns are cut, hedges trimmed and cars washed. Everyone knew everyone, it was like a small village. You really could borrow a cup of sugar from the neighbor.

"Huh?" Duecy replied. He was sharp enough to know the question meant more than the bleak ghetto sights passing outside the window. "Outside, look, what do you see? "He repeated. "Money!" Duecy announced. "I see money. Look at all the junkies!"

"These same junkies use to be teachers, and mailmen, doctors, lawyers... mothers," Carlos replied. "All I see is misery, Misery I fuel everyday, I'm the cause of this."

"What you mean Los? You don't make them use no drugs! If they don't get it from you they gone get it from somewhere! They'll walk to the moon if they had to!"

"They gone have to" Carlos sighed. "Say you ever see a dog use the restroom in his bowl?" "Course not, they gonna go away to do their business, never where they eat" Duecy replied.

"That's right! Only black people do that! You think white people sell drugs in their own neighborhood? Drugs, liquor stores, its crazy." It's not your fault though" Duecy comforts "Sure it is! As long as I contribute to it then it's my fault. I want to quit, but, it's like I have to do. Everyone expects me to be the king" He shakes his head.

"What about the money, power and respect that goes along with it! You the king" Duecy cheers.

"Is that what you think!" Carlos laughs. The notion is so funny it takes a second for him to regain his composure enough to speak. "First of all I don't need the money. My dad was a hood but my mom was a school teacher. She had insurance that made sure I'm straight. Left me my grand fathers barbershop too, I don't need the money, I... hate the money! It's tainted. Power, yeah people move when I tell them but that too is a criminal. There is no honor among thieves, Remember that! You can't trust anyone, your closest people will steal from you if you give them half a chance."

"Meeks took the money didn't he? I could see it in his eyes." Duecy nods.

"Him or Jay, probably both. That means they are plotting against me. You can't trust no one"

"You can trust me! "Duecy swears, "I got yo back!" " I know you do shawty, and I got yours" Carlos laughs as he pulls to a stop at the boarding house Duecy called home. "Hurry up and get your stuff."

Duecy bolts from the car and enters the run-down house. Moments later he emerges with all his worldly possessions stuffed inside black plastic garbage, Carlos knew he couldn't save the world so he would try to save this kid, if no one else.

CHAPTER 5

*C*arlos pulls in front of a well maintained cottage style house and parks. The sight and smell of the colorful rose garden embellishes the quaint front porch. He knows from experience that on a day as beautiful as this the person he is dropping in on would be found in the back yard.

Armed with a handful of roses concealed behind his back he softly enters hoping to surprise her. "Hey mama, how are you doing?" He laughs catching the elderly woman tending to her luscious Red Tomatoes. "Boy! You tryna give me a heart attack!" Mrs. Wright exclaims as she rises to her feet.

"I'm sorry ma'am I didn't mean to scare you" he chuckles leaning down for a well needed hug. "You can't go 'round sneaking up on old folk" she chides and hugs his neck. "Do these make it up?" He asked presenting the flowers." She smiles brightly until she see the roots from where he pulled them out.

"Boy! Did you pull these from my garden!" she asked knowing full well that he did. "My bad mama, I just didn't wasn't to come empty handed." Carlos says apologetically.

"You are too much, come on in this house so I can feed you!" she insist.

Carlos knew she would force feed him and he skipped breakfast for that reason. Mrs. Wright still cooked full course meals for her husband on a daily basis. That was in addition to cleaning, ironing, and what ever else needed to be done. She was maybe the last of a dying breed, old school; take care of your home and your man.

Perhaps men will go back to being men one day and women will once again be their help mates. Perhaps women won't have to pull triple duty of mother, father and bread winner.

Once inside the tidy kitchen Carlos takes a seat in his favorite chair as Mrs. Wright trims the roses to fit into a vase. "So what you doing with yourself boy?" she asks wistfully.

"Same ole same, lil of this lil of that, just tryna eat" Carlos replies and braces himself. A visit to Mrs. Wright wouldn't be complete without a lecture. An ear full to accompany the belly full he was sure to get.

"Hmp! That's what I was afraid of" she began. As she spoke she began removing left over to heat for her guest. She didn't do microwaves, everything would be heated in the oven. That would give her more time to speak with the closest thing to a child she had.

"How long you gonna waste your life in them street?" Until they kill you? Or you trying to see what that pen feels like?" She inquired.

"No ma'am! I have some plans and goals once. Now it seemed so far away.

"After your parents passed and you came here to live with us we had so much hope for your future. You did so well in school. We just knew you were going on to college and then take over the world!" Mrs. Wright moaned. "Boy what happened to your dreams"

"Woke up I guess" Carlos said sadly. "I mean I still have them, I just got side tracked."

"Side tracked? Chile you going backwards! Why you doing that foolishness any how? Your momma made sure you wouldn't want for nothing. Left you the family shop and it's sitting there closed. A trust fund and you in the street with the dinner thieves!"

"I have a little something put up from all this" carols said defensively.

"Chile that hundred grand is a pittance! You gone spend that on a lawyer" she snapped gently.

"How you know what I'm holding? Been in my pockets? Again" Carlos laughed.

"I'm married to your bank remember? 'Sides my husband tells me everything" she said proudly. "We are a team, It us versus them! See that's what you need a good woman! Why you aint got no girlfriend?"

"Cuz my lifestyle I guess. It's hard to know who to trust. I'm about to get out of the game" Carlos announced.

"Game! Is that what you think this is? You think the police is playing? The robbers, them addicts? Aint nobody playing no game!" Mrs. Wright yelled.

"I know momma" Carlos comforts and walks over to embrace the shaking woman. "I feel trapped, I didn't wanna be no king. I'm doing what everyone expects me to do. I'm stuck."

"Boy you aint too big to go 'cross my knee! Forget them fools, be you own man!" "She demands.

"You right. I'm out! Just one more move to make sure everyone is straight."

"Worry about yourself! Carlos your dad talked about quitting all the time. He was making 'one more move' when they murdered him. They will be fine, worry about yourself" Mrs. Wright urged.

"One more move, one more week and I'm out. Gonna turn everything over to Meeks." Mrs. Wright sighs and shakes her head. "So how is Meeks?" I see his momma in church every week. Praying for him as well I bet."

"I'll tell him you asked about him" Carlos advises.

"Don't you lie on me! You wanna tell him something tell him to go check on his momma. Tell him she needs a new roof!" she snaps.

"Well I'm telling him all that! I'ma tell him you said hey!" Carlos laughs. "Tell him to stop by and see you."

"You better not! I never liked that one. Just something about him. Oh! And speaking of church," Mrs., Wright says switching gears. "Boy when you coming back? We aint seen you in a month of Sunday's"

"I stop by every now and then" Carlos says offhandedly.

"I heard. Reverend say he get large amounts of cash err week, think it's you" She says studying him. "How is ole Rev?" Carlos asks dodging the question.

"Ask him yourself, he'll be here any minute" Carlos stuffs the last of his food in his mouth and drains his glass while standing. "Gotta go!" He announces attempting to get out of there before the preacher arrives. "Boy you a mess!" she laughs. Mrs. Wright gives Carlos a firm hug and gentle kiss on his cheek before walking him to the door.

"I really do have to go momma, I have a meeting with a

real estate agent" he announces proudly. "Oh? You buying a house?"

"Nope, they just built a strip mall next to the barber shop. Since I'm planning on opening it back up I figure I may as will open a store too." "That's fantastic!" Mrs. Wright exclaims. "'bout time you leave that foolishness alone."

As she gives him one final hug on the front porch a spanking new luxury car pulls in front of the house. Out steps Reverend Andersen in a designer suite and literally dripping in jewelry. "Speak of the devil!" Carlos chuckles earning a pinch on his arm. "Boy be nice" she warns through clenched teeth.

"Praise the lawd, my two favorite people" the Reverend proclaims as he approaches. "How are you fine people?"

"Fine just fine, how 'bout ya self" Mrs. Wright replies. Carlos forces a smile and nods.

"How bout you" The preacher asks extending his hand. Instead of shaking it Carlos slaps him 'five'.

"Sup Rev. what are those, 22s?" He asked admiring the custom chrome rims on the car.

"Twenty six actually," he replies proudly. "Matter fact you just the man I need to see."

"What you tryna hit the club?" He jokes getting another pinch on the arm

"Let me walk you to your car. Give me one second Mrs. Wright" Reverend Anderson offers.

"See you later momma" Carlos smiles before leaning down to kiss the woman's forehead.

"Ok bye baby, you call me and let me know how things went" she calls behind him.

"I wanna thank you for your generosity" the preacher says as they walk.

"I have no idea what you're talking about "Carlos lies.

"Stacks of cash in the drop box? Tens of thousands? That's not from you huh? Camera aint got your sneaky donations huh?"

"Still nothing" Carlos say shaking his head.

"Well the money is going towards good things I assure you" the preacher says.

"I see" Carlos shouts back looking at the expensive rims on the expensive car. Then the suit, watch and chain.

"So look, we're putting together a trip down to buluxi, bus trip for the church, need a sponsor?"

"A church gambling trip?" Carlos asks incredulously. "Sure why not? It'll be fun, open bar, free food the works!" The preachers say animatedly. "Think I'll pass on this one" Carlos grimaced at the thought.

"Ok I feel you" Anderson nods as Carlos gets into his car. "Holla back about that club, I know a spot."

CHAPTER 6

$\mathcal{P}$art of the Sabir clan, father Ali, mother Amina, and two of the children Hakim and Ruqiyyah are spread out inspecting the potential new location as the agent totes it features.

"This is really a great location!" the agent begins. "Easy access into the lot, ample parking. There is a new sub-division being built nearby so there will be plenty of traffic. Not too mention there are no completing Restaurants with in miles. It's prefect!"

"It is nice" Ali nods inspecting what will be the kitchen.

"Are the other stores leased as of yet? No other food joints are there?" Hakim inquires.

"Yes all the other spots are leased but this one and the one next door. No food... Joints. Just a beauty parlor, laundry mat, video store and I'm meeting a potential tenant shortly who indicated he was opening a clothing store." The agent replies. "That's good look! People will be here for a while so they'll need to eat" Hakim adds.

Meanwhile Ruqiyyah and her mother are planning the

décor and layout of the space. "So what do you ladies think?" Ali asks as he rejoins the group. "I believe this is it Abbi" Ruqiyyah replies eagerly. "It's perfect!"

"I agree" Hakim co-signs. "It is perfect"

"So are you guys ready for this?" Ali asks his children seriously. He knew they were but wanted to hear it from them.

"Yes sir!" They answer in unisom before Hakim steps up. "It's time to expand and I doubt we can find a more suitable location."

"Na'am Abbi, the expressway is close. The colleges are a few miles away, it's a great location" Ruqiyyah adds.

"I'm gonna cry" Amina whines playfully, but a lone tear does manage to escape her eye. "We'll take it" Ali announces to the happy agent.

"Great! Let's sign the lease then" He smiles. "Let me grab the check book" Amina says and rushes outside to their vehicle.

Carlos pulls into the same strip mall and checks the address on the paper. He pulls right next to the Sabir family van and parks. Mrs. Sabir recognizes him and goes over to speak.

"Well hello young man, how are you?" Amina sings filling Carlos mind with memories. This was the sweet lady next door who treated him as one of her own when he was small. The one who held him tightly when his parents were killed.

"Fine, how are you?" Carlos croaked with emotions. "I'm great Al-hamdulillah! the kids and Ali are inside come say hello" she insisted.

"Sure" he replied willing himself to 'man up'. The woman brought back memories he had suppressed long ago. He got his emotions in check and followed her inside. "Hey guys look who I found!" Amina announces as she returns with Carlos in tow. Ruqiyyah does a double take then lowers her gaze.

"Los!" Hakim exclaims and rushes over to embrace his old friend. "How are you?"

"I'm good, good to see you, Mr. Sabir and um, Rosalyn?" Carlos replies causing Ruqiyyah to suppress a smirk.

"It's Ruqiyyah! I'm surprised you don't remember. You were all so close" Mrs. Sabir explains missing the joke. Ali doesn't though.

"Hey Mr. Sabir I see you're already acquainted with your neighbors" The agent pushes hoping to close both deals today. Talk about killing two birds with one stone. It would be an early day.

"You're getting the store next door?" Amina asks, "This is great, we're opening a new restaurant here. Hakim and Ruqiyyah will be running it."

"Cool! You know I can eat you guy's food everyday" Carlos replies.

"Here, let yourself in and have a look around" the agent says handing Carlos the keys. "I'll be over in just a few minutes once I'm done here."

"Ok, thanks" he says accepting the keys, then turns to Sabir's. "Nice seeing you again Mr. and Mrs. Sabir. You too Rolanda."

"Were gonna grab a bite to celebrate if you want to join us "Mr. Sabir offers gruffly.

"I'm fasting Abbi" Ruqiyyah says quickly. "Me too!" Hakim adds causing Amina to frown. "Thanks but I'm tied up today as well" Carlos answers and makes his exit.

"Why you guys fasting so much lately?" the mother asks her children. They both shrug and continue reading the lease. "It's no where near Ramadan." Ali leans in and whispers in his wife ear causing her eyes to grow wide.

"Oh!" She chuckles, "well Masha – Allah! Iftar is on me!"

"Going legit?" Hakim asks as he enters the empty unit. "Been legit" Carlos says embarrassed.

"Is that right?" Hakim asks lifting the crown from his chest, "Just cuz I aint in the streets don't mean I don't hear what's going on. I hear you're the king"

"Don't believe everything you hear" he replies pulling the medallion away. "I'm out! Be sure your sister knows that too."

"My sister? Man you still sweating Ruqiyyah "he laughs. "Don't waste your time, one she got brothers hounding my pops about her and two you aint Muslim"

"so she aint got a man then?" Carlos asks undeterred.

"You crazy! We need to link up. Ummi said to bring you to the masjid" Hakim relays.

"That's a bet, man I aint been there in forever!" Carlos reflects. Being so close to the Sabir family as a child he was a frequent visitor to their masjid. He has a ton of joyful memories about the place. The one thing that still stood out was the calm. It was the most peaceful place on the planet.

"*A*ight I'll holla then, as Salaam aslaykum" "Yeah salaam and bacon to you too" Carol laughs.

"So what do you think?" the agent asks entering as Hakim exits.

"I'll take it!"

CHAPTER 7

"You can't check me!" Duecy brags then crossing his opponent over and proves it with a pretty finger roll. "He served you!" Vic another teen instigates. It's the first time Duecy got to see his friends from the block since he left.

They all met up at the park for hoops and trash talk. Duecy squints his eyes as he watches Rips custom truck pull up next to where Meeks is parked.

"Thought yall was beefing with those guys?" Robert asks as the two supposed enemies share hand shakes. "Thought we was too?" Duecy replies. "I'll find out when I get home.

"Where you staying now? I went by the rooming house, they said you moved" Vic inquires. "I moved in with Los" he said proudly. "He making me ready for that crown." The lie was better than the truth of being enrolled and excelling in school. Somehow black society has detiorated to the point where education was scorned. It was cool to be dumb.

"What you his girl or something?" Reggie the 'hater of the group quips . He hated all things positive.

"Hey just cuz I'm in school don't make me soft watch your mouth" Duecy warned.

"I'm just saying, aint no money in school" Reggie added.

"I'm straight Los got a job for me" Duecy said

"Put me on!'" go back to school too!" Vic begged.

"Me too!" Robert yelled.

"Man yall tripping. Aint no money in school, why I want an allowance when I can grind for mines!" Reggie gripes and storms off taking all the negative energy with him.

"Anyway, my ball." Robert announces and resumes play. Duecy watches curiously as Rip and Meeks talk like old friends.

"It's all set for Friday" Rip begins "we're making a big buy so be ready. I'll stop buy the flea market, you guys do it then. Dave will be with you to make sure it goes down correctly. Rico's not going to make it".

"Dave? What don't trust me?" Meeks ask.

"No, not for a second" Rip laughs."

"That's cool cuz Mike will be with you when you guys hit the bank. Make sure Carlos goes with Rico" Meeks plots.

❄

"We went to the new store the other day! We're going to get it!" Ruqiyyah informs her best friend during a rare lull in customers.

"Ooh I'm so happy for you guys! Alhamdulillah!" Hanifa rejoices and hugs her. "I know yall got a job for a sister, especially when Hakim finally marries me!"

"I don't know bout either of them!" Ruqiyyah teases. "For real though I know Hakim likes you, I think you scare him."

"Me! How?" she said loud enough to cause Ali to stick his head out.

"That's how!" Ruqiyyah laughs, "You're so... so... loud! My brother is laid back"

"I'll be quiet! Promise" she says just as loudly. Causing them both to crack up. That's how Hakim finds them when he enters.

"As Salaamu as salaam" He greets cheerfully. "Wa Alaykum as salaam" they sing together. "I'm heading over to the new store, they are supposed to deliver the coolers" Hakim advises. "Insha-allah, do you need any help?" Ruqiyyah ask.

"Yeah, we can come if you want" Hanifa offers, "nah, I'm cool. I'm meeting Carlos over there, you know he been asking about you" he adds. "Oh he did get the store huh?" Ruqiyyah asked ignoring the statement.

"The same Carlos who was in here?" Hanifa inquired feeling left out.

"He's opening a clothing store so we're talking about doing some cross promotions. Radio, flyers and stuff. Maybe coupons or something."

"Sounds good. Do your thing bruh, tell what's his face, then again" Ruqiyyah stops short. "Tell him yo-self at Jumu'ah, ummi made him come" Hakim said and turns to leave.

"You sure you don't need me to come" Hanifa calls to his back as he departs the store. "Hard to get remember? Try ignoring him" "anyway, so thats the one!" Hanifa says excitedly.

"One what?" Ruqiyyah asks frowning. "You said you wouldn't talk to Carlos cuz one he's not Muslim, he coming to Jumu'ah!"

"Still gotta get past Abbi, and my father is no joke!"

✳

"Ok, I want the Falcons logo right in the middle" Carlos instructs the paint crew, He decided each wall of the store would feature murals of Atlanta sport franchises to cater to the chosen demographic. "What's up shawty?" Hakim drawls upon entering Carlos's store.

"Shawty? What's up? What happen to Salaami and bacon" Carlos jokes as he goes to embrace his friend. "Just trying to speak your language "Hakim replies, "looking good! Where you putting the Giants?".

"Wont be no Giants in here! Strictly A.T.L!" Carlos says proudly.

"No matter how much they lose huh? Anyway the coolers should be coming today. Did you talk to the brother about the display counter?"

"Yeah! Man you saved me a ton of money!" Carlos exclaimed happily.

"That's the Muslim connection son! We got a whole network, Doctors, lawyers, painters you name it" Hakim explains. "Excuse me" One of the painters asks politely. "I see you Moozlum, can you tell me what a bean pie and a bow tie got to do with God?"

"Good question, I'm Muslim! I can't tell you" Hakim answers politely despite feeling slighted.

"That's the nation" Carlos interjects. "They aint Muslims. They don't follow Qur'an and Sunnah" Hakim nods with approval at the correct answer and Carlos's coming to his aid.

"So what's the difference?" The painter asks contritely.

"Like he said, we Muslims follow the Qur'an which is the revealed speach of God as well the example of his last and final prophet to mankind, Muhammad may the peace and blessing of Allah be upon him." Hakim explained.

"So do yall pray to Muhammad?" the painter asked.

"The prophet, peace and blessing of Allah be upon him was a man, a prophet. We follow his way but we don't pray to or through him" Hakim answers.

"Yall got a hard religion" the painter says shaking his head.

"It's a complete way of life. Every aspect of the day relates to worship." Carlos adds.

"Well, I can't give up my pork! I got a pork chop sandwich in the truck right now!, pork skins and bacon!" The painter announces and gets back to work.

"I see you haven't forgotten" Hakim tells Carlos.

"How could I, it's embedded in my soul" he replies.

"Then act upon it!"

CHAPTER 8

*a*s soon as Carlos turns the door knob to enter his house Duecy drops the game controller and jumps up to greet him.

"What's up Los! How was your day?" He asks so eagerly he's practically bouncing up and down.

"Why you so happy to see me, what you break something or something?" Carlos replies playfully. "Nah! Just had a good day at school!"

"Oh yeah, what was so good?" Carlos asked grabbing the controller and resuming Duecy's game.

"Everything! Man it was so cool just learning again!" He exclaimed. "No police, no robbers, no drama!"

"Told you"Carlos said proudly. "Say, did you tell the other kids about the deal?"

"Yeah I told them. Vic and Robert said they down, but Reggie …" Duecy replied shaking his head. He knew his friend was stupid but this was far beyond. Carlos offered them legit jobs in exchange for going back to school. Who wouldn't want a deal like that.

. . .

"*D*oes he know he's cut off if he doesn't take the offer? Carlos asked hotly.

"He knows. Said he'll just work for Rico dem" Ducey replied. "Oh! I forgot to tell you! I seen Meeks meeting with Rip in the park!

"When?" Carlos asks intently. "Just them two? Rico wasn't with them?"

"Nope just Rip and Meeks. Had a nice long talk about something."

Carlos knew he was the subject of that conversation and knew Meeks must be planning to cross him, He just wondered when?

"Did he see you?" Carlos inquired, plotting himself. "No" Duecy replies, reaching to take his game back. "Good, makes sure you don't say anything to him about it. He's on his way over. Finish your homework and them you can go play" Carlos laughs swatting his hand away from the controller.

❄

"*S*o it's all set huh?" Jay asks Meeks almost remorsefully. "You sure you can trust this dude Rip?"

"I don't even trust my on momma!" Meeks replies truthfully. The dirty business in which he has spent most of his life had turned his heart completely black. He could now commit sins and crimes without the slightest trace of remorse. He just didn't care about anything, or anyone anymore.

"But Carlos man! We go so far back!" Jay protest.

"This is business, not personal!" Meeks barks!" Do you have any idea how much money is getting by us? We could all be rich by now".

"I feel that. It's like Los don't want the money! Real talk, dude is just going through the motions"

"That's cuz he already got paper!" Meeks spits jealousy. "He got like two fifty in a trust fund from when his people died. Not too mention a barber shop a house, he's straight! We the ones struggling!"

Jay shot a glance around the sixty thousand dollar truck out fitted with thirty thousand more in extra's at the struggling remark. They were far from struggling. Greedy is more like it.

"Well that explains why he act the way he do. We could be seeing a lot more money. Yeah it might be better if he wasn't around" Jay gives in.

"Well it's going down on Friday" Meeks says. He leaves out the part about hitting the bank. Friday was when Carlos made his deposits.

❄

"They moved the buy until two on Friday", Rip tells his boss, luring him into the well planned trap.

"We gonna be ok until then?" Rico ask curing about the change in plans.

"Yeah we'll just make it, only you gotta make the run with me cuz Mike can't make it" Rio adds firmly placing the noose around his bosses neck.

"No problem, be nice to get back onto the trenches for

minute" He agrees securing his fate. "Once we get our warehouse full we'll be ready to move on Carlos. That crown is about to come home to where it belongs. I'm the king!"

CHAPTER 9

*C*arlos has half his closet laid out on his be trying to decide on what to wear to the masjid. It had been so long he almost forgot. When he went to live with the Wrights he had to go to church with them. He always wore suits and ties and remembers the stuffy, uncomfortable feel of them.

In the end he settled on a pair of plain slacks, polo shirt and loafers. Out of sheer habit he places the gaudy crown around his neck.

"Nah" Carlos chides himself and places the chain and medallion on his coffee table as he goes to answer the door bell.

"ooh dat knock pon mi door" Carlos calls out in a mock Caribbean accent. "It's me Ms. Cleo, now open up!" Hakim calls out from the other side.

"Salami and bacon" Carlos teases as he opens the door.

"You better get that out your system before you get to the masjid of somebody might beat you up. Like ummi!" Hakim says as they embrace.

"Hey you remember when your mom tore both of us up!" Carlos recalled fondly.

"Do I! Got me in trouble following behind you!"

"Um no, that was your idea remember!" Carlos shot back.

"Anyway!" Hakim laughs, knowing he's right. "Are you ready?"

"Yep can't wait. I gotta stop by the store after so I'll follow you, Carlos replies.

"Me too, got contractors coming to install the deep fryers, so you may as well ride with me" Hakim says. The two men ride across town to the masjid in silence. Both consumed with their own thought until Carlos finally voices his.

"Say bro, you think your sister would marry me if I was Muslim?" He asked plainly. Hakim shoots a glance over to his friend to see if he is serious. When he sees that he is he thinks for a few seconds more before responding.

"It was reported by Umar, may Allah be pleased with him, that Allah's messenger, peace and blessing be upon him said, actions are only by intentions, and every man has only what he intends. Whoever migrates for Allah and his messenger then his migration is for Allah and his messenger, Whoever migrates for some worldly gain of to acquire a woman he will marry then his migration is for that" Hakim quoted.

"If I were to 'migrate' it wouldn't be for in a woman."Carlos replies emphatically.

"Allah knows best" Hakim answers. "But glad to see your head is in the right direction. One becoming Muslim and two finding a wife. The prophet peace be upon him said marriage is half of your religion."

"So why you aint got married yet then" Carlos inquired.

"Haven't met the right sister yet, plus I'm so busy with the store it wouldn't be fair "He answered.

"So what about when you feel... manly?"

"Manly?" Hakim laughs, "I fast! Dang near everyday!"

"Yeah you are looking a little thin" Carlos laughs. "What about that sister who works with Ru?"

"Who Hanifa!" Hakim exclaims, "She a good sister, knows the religion, covers and prays, just... loud"

"What about for me?" Carlos asks suppressing a smirk. He knows his friend will enough to hear what he didn't say.

"For you! Nah, the sister is taken!" He said firmly having just decided that he would take her.

"Pretty much what I thought," Carlos chuckles. The mood goes from festive to solemn as they pull into the crowded masjid parking lot. Hakim following the deputy hired to control traffic flow direction and parks. They walk quietly into the building.

Hakim leads the way to the restroom and watches proudly as his friend perform ablution. "See you remember how to make wudu huh?"

"I never stopped. I've been doing this since your dad taught us back in the days. "He replied.

The call to prayer is being chanted beautifully as they emerge from the restroom so they hasten to the musallah, Carlos sits Indian style on the plush carpet as Hakim performs two cycles of prayer before joining him.

The Imam walks out and greets the people and begins. After opening in Arabic he translate into English and starts his sermon.

"All praise and thanks is for Allah, we seek is aid and help, and forgiveness. I seek refuge with Allah from the evils of my own self and the badness of my deeds.

I bear witness that none has the right to be worshipped but Allah and that Muhammad peace be upon him is his messenger. Who ever Allah guides is rightly guided and whoever Allah allows to stray none can guide.

Oh you, who believe, fear Allah as he should be feared and die not except in a state of submission to him. And how can you die as a Muslim if you refuse to live as one?

And I use the word 'refuse' because that's what you do! No one has to tell you the difference between right and wrong. You already know, yet choose to do wrong!

In Surah Ibrahim, Ayat twenty four Allah the most high gives the parable of faith as a beautiful tree, its roots are firmly established and its branches tower to the sky.

The tree, the tree of faith, Eman gives its fruit at all times. This is just like Eman, its roots are firmly established and it gives its fruit at all times.

Once Eman, faith enters the heart it can never leave. It may decrease but it never leaves. It may go down to the point where a person falls into sins or bad deeds. So much so that a person stops acting upon it, stops praying, ect, but it never leaves.

Islam, Eman is a one way street! People of all ages, races, backgrounds are flocking to Islam once it's been accepted by the heart it can never leave.

When you see a person renounce Islam or leave, you will see that Islam, Eman had never entered his heart. He or she may have been born into Muslim family or raised in a Muslim country and just went along but faith never entered their heart. Once Eman enters the heart it never leaves. Its roots are firmly established. Its branches reach to the sky!

The tree of Eman is not a small tree, its not hidden or concealed, when a person has Eman everyone around him will see it. He or she becomes a land mark through whom others are judged. Your faith, Eman makes you right, just, and decent people. It affects his speech, manners and dealing with people.

This tree gives its fruit at all times by the permission of it lord. Other trees produce their fruit seasonally, one a year, twice a year, but no other tree gives its fruit at all times except the tree of Eman. Eman benefits you at all times.

And what are the fruits of faith? The greatest fruit of this is of course paradise! Allah, the mighty and majestic said, 'Those who believe and do good deeds shall have Jennah as a place of residence.' Eman is the key to paradise.

Whoever has Eman will enter Jennah and whoever does not will never enter it, faith, Eman is a protection from the fire of hell.

The person who has the bare minimum of Eman will not enter hell. It is not possible. If he of she does the obligatory acts and avoids the major sins. When one has this minimum then hell is forbidden to him.

But the beauty of Eman is that even if you have less than the minimum amount of Eman, as long as there is some Eman he will not remain in the hell fire.

The prophet peace and blessing upon him said; 'A group of people who had Eman the size of a coin will be taken out of the fire. Then another group who had Eman the weight of a leaf will be taken out. Then another batch who had Eman the weight of a mustard seed, then another who had just tiniest trace of Eman will be removed from the fire, until the only people who remain are those who had no Eman at all! The faithless.

Eman is also a means of being forgiveness for our sins and evil deeds. Allah says in the Qur'an 'as for the one who repents, has Eman and does good deeds the Allah will exchange his evil deeds with good ones!'

Eman acts as an exit, an escape from all sorrow and problems. Allah the most high said; 'whoever has fear of him, he will make a way out from every difficulty.'

Eman gives you status, People see it and respect you. Look up to you. You become their role models. They expect nothing but good from you. They confide in you and seek your guidance and approval.

Now Eman can not be restricted to the heart. It must be acted upon. Think back to the verses of Qur'an I quoted, 'those who believe and do good deeds!' Eman is action!

If not then the devil would be a believer! He believes in Allah, the Qur'an, the Prophet peace be upon him, but where are his good deeds? Where are yours?

Eman starts in the heart but it must move on to the tongue in the form of shahadah, testifying that there is no god but Allah and Muhammad is his messenger. In remembering Allah, calling to Allah, and reciting the Qur'an. Then it must move on to the limbs in the form of the five daily prayers, charity, fasting and doing good deeds.

Eman has a taste and it's sweet. Three things show when a person has tasted the sweetness of Eman. They are being pleased with Allah as his lord, and Muhammad as his prophet as Islam as his way of life."

The Imam then sat and made a prayer between the two halves of the sermon. Carlos was so struck on the first half he missed the second. He sat reflecting on his life in conjunction with what he just heard. The contradiction forced tears to trickle down his face. Since this wasn't the time or place to 'man up' he allowed them to flow. He was forced back into the present when everyone began lining up to pray. Having prayed so many times before as a child he knew just what to do and got into the rows.

To his surprise he actually remembered all the words. It was if they were etched on his heart, or was that Eman?

"Well, what did you think?" Hakim asked his friend once they made it out into the lobby.

"I think I'm a Muslim. I felt like he was talking directly to me. He was!" Carlos replied.

"Al-hamdul-lillah! You ready to take Shahadah?"

"Not just yet" Carlos frowned. "There's one more thing I need to handle."

"Die not except in a state of submission" Hakim reminded. Before Carlos could respond Amina and Ruqiyyah approached.

"As salaamu alaykum young men" Mrs. Sabir greeted warmly.

"Wa alykum as salaam ummi" Hakim replies quickly before Carlos could salami and bacon them.

"As salaamu alaykum Mrs. Sabir, Rolanda" Carlos smiles. Ruqiyyah rolls her eyes and turns away as Hakim cracks up. Amina looks at all of them wondering what she missed.

"Did you enjoy the Khutbah?" Mrs. Sabir asked. "Loved it! It changed my life. I will definitely be back" Carlos exclaimed.

"Insha Allah" the Sabir clan said together.

"Carlos wants to take his Shahadah... next week" Hakim tells. "Next week? Child how do you know there will be a next week?" Mrs. Sabir asks. Ruqiyyah even turns to hear the answer to this.

"Have a few things to handle, "he offered meekly.

"Don't die except for as a Muslim." Amina advised.

"I keep hearing that" Carlos replies stoically. They

exchange the greeting once more and the women leave. Carlos wanders into the masjid book store while Hakim goes and offers a few more cycle of prayer.

As salaamu Alaykum! Its good to see you again. Especially here!" a vaugely familar man says pulling a confused Carlos into a bear hug.

"Um Wa alaykum salaam" he replies, trying to place the strangers face.

"You don't remember me do you? He asked upon releasing him.

"I can't say that I do" Carlos said after studying his face. "You kinda look familiar though."

"I'm Sa'id, I was a friend of your father, and you look just like him" Sa'id said through a smile.

"Oh ok" Carlos said not sure what more to day.

"I saw them working on the shop, did you guys sell it?"

"No, I'm opening a store in the new strip mall across the street too. Heading down there now" Carlos replies proudly.

"I'll stop by, I wanna check the place out" Sa'id offers.

"Insha Allah" Carlos replied happy to have a chance to apply his new phrase. "Insha Allah, As-salaamu alsykum."

CHAPTER 10

"*L*et's make a quick stop at the flea market" Rip suggests pulling off of the main street into the parking lot.

"Now! With all that in the trunk?" Rico ask from the passenger side. "Can't it wait?"

"Only be a sec" Rip replies pulling into the spot of ambush. What he doesn't know is the plans been changed.

At the same across town Duecy is closing in on a new record. He is so engrossed in his video game he ignores the phone letting it go to voice mail instead.

"Hey Carlos this is Carl, called your cell phone but its off. Look I'm leaving shortly so if you plan on making your deposit you better hurry." Mr. Wright says onto the recording.

The message springs young Duecy into action. The first order of business was to pause his game and preserve the record he just broke. It was Carlos's long standing record and he couldn't wait to show off.

He rushed into the room Carlos used as an office and

sure enough the bag containing the weekly proceeds was on the floor. Duecy grabbed the bag and the key Carlos's truck. He had just gotten his license and knew he wouldn't mind.

As Duecy rushed through the living room he spied the crown laying off the coffee table. He reasoned that since he was on kings business it would only be right to wear it.

※

"*W*here are you?" Meeks asked when D.C. answered his phone.

"Me and Jay at the store waiting on the move" he replied. "There has been a change in plans. Leave Jay there with Carlos and the old man! "He said ominously.

"*T*hat's what's up" D.C agreed quickly. His heart was covered by a black stain that made deeds such as the one he was about to commit seem fair. "Here come the truck now."

"Handle that, the money splits two ways a lot better than three" Meeks said and hung up.

D.C decided to use Carlos truck for his get away and 'left' Rip in his own. Once he saw a man enter the store wearing the crown and carrying the tote bag that had been described he took off behind them.

Back at the flea market Meeks other plan had been carried out and population of the earth decreased by two, but there was more to come.

※

*C*arlos is engrossed in his new Qur'an when in walks Sa'id into the clothing store. "As salaamu alaykum, good book you got there" Sa'id greets upon entering.

"Wa alaykum as-salaam, great book! I have a million and one questions though" Carlos replies.

"I know the feeling, be patient little brother" he responds. "I went over to the shop and the contractor said you were over here."

"Yeah I'm doing a lot at once" Carlos admitted. He knows the key to a successful business was work. "So how did you know my dad?"

"Oh we go way back! Use to work together," "work? My father never has a …. Oh! Work! Carlos caught on. "Yeah that was a life time ago" Sa'id says wishfully.

"So where were you when my dad …. You know?"

"Oh I was out by then! I never really had the heart for it, lives were being lost, people were going to jail. Carl was facing a hundred years, but paid the right people and only did one"he explained answering the question to where Mr. Wright was when Carlos first went to live at his house. For the first year of life with the Wright's Mr Wright was absent.

"So I just quit, Told your dad I was out and that was that!" Sa'id said emphatically "walked away!"

"Just like that? Just walked away? From the money the power, the …"

"Problem, the danger, the sin! Yep, just walked away" Sa'id cut in. "I took that silly crown off and walked away."

"Crown! You were one of the three kings?" Carlos asks incredulously. He knew he had gave up the world if he was one of the kings.

"That's what we called ourselves" Sa'id laughed showing

just how foolish the concept was. They were death merchants who sold poison, not kings. "Your father wanted to quit, talked about it all the time. He said he was trapped, had too many people counting on him. He finally said he was out, wanted one more score to make sure his workers were ok and, well, you know how that turned out."

"Not too well" Carlos agreed.

"He knew he wouldn't make it. Made me promise to look after you, if anything happened to him. I always checked on you through Mr. Wright; saw you at his store a few times. You had that crown on looking just like your dad."

"So why didn't you say something? Tell me to quit too?" Carlos pleaded.

"Like I said, you had that crown on. You wouldn't have heard me" Sa'id advised.

"Yeah you might be right" Carlos nods, and clutches his Qur'an. "A lot has changed since then."

"I see! So are you Muslim now? "He asked eagerly.

"Um…. Well… I have some things to do first. I have to make sure. My people… I know that's where I belong. Everyone was so nice."

"I know. When I quit that say I ended up there somehow. Been there ever since." Sa'id said. "Walked away a hero! Tell your people to keep what ever is in the streets, you won't need it. Allah will suffice you. Turn to Surah 4 Ayat 100"

Carlos quickly flips to the chapter and verse smiling as he reads it. "He who emigrates in the cause of Allah will find on earth many dwelling places and plenty to live by."

"In other words you'll be alright" Sa'id urges. The two men exchanges hugs and greeting of peace as Sa'id departs. Sometime later Hakim enters and finds Carlos stick stuck deep into his Qur'an.

"As salaamu alaykum, I've been calling, your phone is off!" He announces as he approaches. "My bad, it's been off all day. Need a break, feel me?" Carlos replies. He pulls his phone out his pocket but then puts it back without turning it back on.

"Let's go home" Hakim suggests and leads the way to his car.

CHAPTER 11

"*I* know he better bring It back washed, waxed and with a full tank!" Carlos announced as Hakim pulled into the space his truck should be parked in. "Kids Hakim laughs at his predicament. "At least your getting some hands on daddy practice."

"Speaking of which, tell your …. Nah, never mind"

"I'll tell her Hakim laughs and pulls out of the driveway. Once inside Carlos finally turns his phone on. The intention was to text Meeks and abdicate the throne, his decision was made. He quit!

The phone began vibrating wildly from the influx of text and voice messages that had accumulated while the phone was off. The blinking light on his answering caught his attention. When he hit play Mrs. Wrights frantically shill voice filled the room.

"Carlos! Carlos! Where are you! Carl got robbed, he's hurt! Get down to the hospital now!"

That's exactly what he did. Carlos flew downtown and

rushed into the emergency room waiting room. That's where he found Mrs. Wright with her face buried in her hands. Her demeanor stopped him in his tracks. "Momma" he called out tentatively as he approached. She sprang up and into his arms weeping.

"Is he ok?" Carlos asked and held his breath awaiting an answer. The waiting room was crawling with police officers. That was a bad sign.

"He's ok, he had on that vest you gave him" she sniffled and paused. Carlos felt her squeeze him tighter and knew grim news was to follow. "The little boy, the one you sent to make the deposit" she began.

"Who? I didn't send anyone" he replied. "He had on your chain. They took it, he didn't make it baby" she said breaking down. "Excuse me" a detective said cutting into his grief." I need a word with you." Reluctantly Carlos releases the old woman and steps to the side with the detective. As bad as the situation was what the police told him made it even worse.

"One person survived, a Jason Elder" He began. It had been so long since Carlos heard Jays given mane it took a second to process.

"He won't walk again but he'll live. He gave a statement that you were the intended victim. The kid just was in the wrong place at the wrong time. Why would they target you?"

"I'm hearing this for the first time. Your guess is as good as mines" Carlos replied.

"He says Meeks set it up as well as a similar situation on memorial drive" The detective said.

Carlos couldn't take anymore. His knees buckled and it was all he could to stay upright. He never cared about the money so he didn't mourn its loss. He did miss Duecy already. If not for final exams that morning he would have been at the masjid with him.

"Where are you going?" The detective inquired as Carlos began to slowly walk away. "At least take my card"

He didn't, he kept on walking to his car. He then drove home where he stayed for the next month. No phone, T.V. or human contact for a month just him, his Qur'an and new pass-time salat.

❄

*J*ay survived the attack in tact minus the ability to walk. He could talk though which meant Meeks would spend the rest of his days in prison. There would be no crown for him.

During this same time Hakim finally asked Hanifa to marry him after a few minutes of giggles between her and Ruqiyyah she accepted. The Nikka was set for Friday after the Salatul – Jumu'ah.

No one paid any attention when Carlos walked into the musallah since the Khutbah was underway. He offered the customary two cycles of prayer and sat down. He missed most of the talk by arriving late as well as being consumed by his thoughts.

Carlos lined up in the ranks and prayed with the congregation. As usual several people stood up after the prayer to make the testimony of faith and become Muslim. The now bearded Carlos was first.

"Is that?" Ruqiyyah asked squinting to make sure her eyes weren't playing tricks on her.

"It is!" Hanifa cheered as they drew near. Hakim was

smiles as he saw his friend stand in front of the Iman and repeat. "Ash-hado ana illaha Illallah, wa ash-hado anna muhammadar-rasodlullah" He offered proudly. Then translated.

"I Bear witness that none has the right to be worshipped but Allah and Muhammad may the peace and blessing of Allah be upon him, is his messenger!"

He was greeted by all the brothers around him with handshakes, hugs and the greeting of peace. When he saw Ruqiyyah smiling face he went to her. "As salaamu alaykum sister" he offered looking at her socks.

"Wa alaykum as salaam" she replied shyly. "Um, I can I, I mean" Carlos stammered. He took a deep breath and forced the words out. "I need to speak with your father, your wali. I want you to be my wife."

"ABBIiii!!!" Ruqiyyah screamed alerting everyone. When they saw the wall to wall smile she wore they already knew.

"Yes my daughter?" Ali asked formally while looking as Carlos.

"The brother just asked me to marry him!" She said giddily from the excitement.

"And?" He replied. The Sabir patriarch knew his children well and trusted their judgment. She nodded enthusiastically, covering her smile with her hand. Her nod would have been enough but he still looked towards his son as well. When Hakim gave his approval with a nod of his own he turned to his future son in law.

"As salaamu alaykum ibn. I looked at you as a son when you were young and now, you are my son, take care of my daughter" Ali said firmly.

"Wa alaykum as salaam," Carlos replied accepting his out stretched hand. "Insha Allah."

As salaamu alaykum.

The two couples married in a joint ceremony a few weeks later lived happily ever after, but that's part two.

GLOSSARY

- Allah : This is the Arabic word used by both Christians and Muslims meaning one God.
- Abbi : the Arabic word for father.
- Al hamdulillah: this means that ALL praise is for God.
- Ayat : a verse from the Quran
- As salaamu alaykum : peace be unto you
- Eman : faith
- Imam: Muslim spiritual leader.
- Ibn : son
- Insha Allah: God willing
- Islam : Is the way of life practiced by 1.5 billion people. It is not a religion but a complete way of life.
- Jennah : Arabic for Paradise
- Jumu'ah: linguisticaly means Friday but more often used to refer to Friday prayers which are obligatory for Muslim males to attend.

- Khutbah: religious talk or sermon
- Muslim : any person who practices Islam as his or her way of life.
- Musallah: place of prayer
- Quran : the. Muslims holy book
- Salat : the five daily prayers obligatory on all Muslims past puberty male or female.
- Shahadah : It is that you pledge a covenant with Allah (God), the Creator of the heavens and earth, the ruler of all that exist, the Lord of majesty and Honor that nothing has the right to be worshipped but God and that Muhammad is his messenger.
- Surah : chapter of the Quran
- Taqwa: God consciousness
- Ummi : Arabic for my mother
- Wali : is a male guardian for unmarried women. Could be father, brother, son or other male relative

www.ingramcontent.com/pod-product-compliance
Lightning Source LLC
Chambersburg PA
CBHW060451280326
41933CB00014B/2728

* 9 7 8 1 9 5 2 5 4 1 5 1 3 *